The
HAUNTING
of
Cassie Palmer

The
HAUNTING
of
Cassie Palmer

VIVIEN ALCOCK

MAMMOTH

TO LEON AND JANE

First published in Great Britain 1980
by Methuen Children's Books Ltd
Published 1991 by Mammoth
an imprint of Reed International Books Ltd
Michelin House, 81 Fulham Road, London sw3 6rb
and Auckland, Melbourne, Singapore and Toronto

Reprinted 1994 (twice), 1996

Copyright © 1980 Vivien Alcock

ISBN 0 7497 0708 9

A CIP catalogue record for this title
is available from the British Library

Printed and bound in Great Britain
by Cox & Wyman Ltd, Reading, Berkshire

One

Cassie was walking home in the rain. People sheltering in shop doorways turned to watch her. Figures blinded by their own umbrellas bumped into her, muttered apologies, and tilted their umbrellas to stare after her. With her wet hair streaking her cheeks like spilled paint and her shoes squelching at every step, she was strolling down the shining pavements as if it were high dry summer. She wasn't showing off, she just did not want to go home.

If I'd any money, I'd run away! she thought bitterly, but there was only a penny in her pocket. A lighted bus hissed by, filled with people glad to be going home. Late shopkeepers locked their doors, turned up their coat collars and hurried home. Everyone was hurrying home, except her. She didn't want to go home. Not tonight. Tom was going to a party. Mary was staying the night with a friend of hers. But *she* was ordered to come straight home, not for a punishment, not even to do anything – except go up to her room two hours early and keep as quiet as a mouse.

'Why can't *I* go out?' she'd asked. 'It's not as if you let me take part –'

'Just your being in the house may help, Cassandra,' her mother had said mysteriously.

She was always Cassandra on Friday nights. Cassie was good enough for the rest of the week, but on Fridays nothing but her full name would do. Cassandra Palmer, seventh child of a seventh child, and therefore credited, by the strange arithmetic of Mrs Palmer's world, with the gift of second sight. Not that it showed yet, but Mrs Palmer wasn't worried. 'It'll come when it's good and ready,' she'd say comfortingly, as if she thought Cassie wanted to see things that weren't there, and go round foretelling doom and disaster at the drop of a tea-leaf! She didn't. It was hardly the kind of thing to spread happiness and gain popularity, was it? She hated ghosts. She did not even believe in them.

I've a good mind to stop out all night and catch pneumonia, she thought, but went on walking. Down Spenser Street, cross by the lights, left into Marlowe Drive, up Chaucer Avenue and there she was, very wet, very cold and very sad at heart. Shakespeare Street. A dull little street running between dull little houses. Number 11 was somewhat larger than its neighbours, with a small garden and a high hedge all around it, giving them, her mother said, the privacy they needed. Home.

Mrs Palmer was not in the kitchen. Nor in the

living-room. Cassie went to the foot of the stairs. 'Mum?'

'Is that you, Cassandra? You're late!'

'It's raining.'

'Never mind, have your supper quickly. It's on the table.'

'I'm all wet!'

She heard the bathroom door open and a towel came flying down the stairs. Then the door shut again.

'Oh thanks,' muttered Cassie, picking the towel up. She stood wrapping it in a turban round her wet hair and staring moodily at the door opposite. I'm cold, she thought, that's why I'm shivering. Anyone would shiver who was as cold and as wet as me. It doesn't mean I'm afraid. There's nothing in there to be afraid of.

She opened the door and looked in. Her mother had left the light on but so thick was its shade and so weak the bulb it enclosed that the room seemed full of shadows. But that was all they were, shadows. If at times they seemed to move, it must be because there was a window open behind the long crimson curtains. And the odd, earthy smell was just the white chrysanthemums on the sideboard. There was nothing alarming in the cold, rather bleak room. As it was Friday, the crystal ball had been put away in its wooden case and the crimson velvet cloth removed from the round table. Seven wooden chairs were arranged around this, crowded together to make

7

room for the wing-chair facing the door. Her mother's chair. One day destined to be hers.

I don't want any part of it, thought Cassie. I'll abdicate. I never asked to be the seventh child. Sometimes I wish she'd stopped at six! She's no right to count on me. I must tell her. Oh why am I so feeble? I'll tell her tonight –

Her mother walked very lightly for such a large woman. She was half-way down the stairs before Cassie heard her.

'What are you doing, Cassandra?'

'Just looking.'

'You haven't touched anything?'

'No. I haven't been in.'

'Good girl,' said her mother, but her eyes checked quickly round the room before she shut the door. 'Come along, now, Cassie,' she said, taking Cassie by the shoulders and pushing her into the kitchen. 'You're late enough already.'

'I hate Fridays,' said Cassie. She caught sight of the plate of ham sandwiches and mug of milk left out for her. 'I *hate* Fridays,' she repeated.

'It's only one day a week, that's not too much to ask, is it? Do get a move on. At this rate they'll be here before you're upstairs, and you know I need some time to myself. A little peace and quiet to collect my powers . . . to recharge myself. Oh, it's not so easy, my girl, as you'll find out when your time comes.'

'Mum –'

'Somehow I feel all on edge tonight.' Mrs Palmer fidgeted in front of the mirror. 'Do I look all right?'

Cassie glanced at her. Mrs Palmer was wearing her black velvet dress, fastened at the neck by a small gold brooch and then falling down over her ample curves until it reached the cat's water bowl on the floor. She looked very large, and in such a small kitchen, rather overpowering, but in her daughter's eyes at least, there was something rather splendid about her.

'You've got too much powder on,' Cassie said. 'You look like you've buried your head in a bag of flour and only just been resurrected. Otherwise you're fine. Who's coming tonight? The usual bunch?'

'One extra. Mrs Huntley Brown is bringing her nephew.'

So that's why her mother was nervous. She always was on edge when someone new came. 'It's Friday the thirteenth,' said Cassie, looking at the calendar on the wall by the stove.

'I know,' said her mother uneasily, appearing none too pleased to have been reminded of it. 'Lucky for some,' she added hopefully.

'I'm thirteen, too,' said Cassie.

'Lucky for you, I hope. What did you want to be, twelve?'

Cassie was silent. This obviously was not the right night to tell her mother that she did not want to follow in her footsteps. In fact, she was beginning to

9

wonder if it was the right night for anything. It had an unlucky feel to it somehow.

'Mum, cancel it tonight! Tell 'em not to come!'

Her mother stared at her in astonishment. 'Cassie, what's all this? How can I?'

'You could say I was ill.'

'I don't like to do that. I never have. I always feel – anyway,' she said, looking at her watch, 'it's too late. Some of them live right the other side of town. They'll have set out already. You're *not* ill, are you?' She laid a large hand on Cassie's forehead. 'Quite cool. You're pale, but then you always are. Your eyes are bright enough.' A sudden thought struck her and her own eyes brightened. 'Cassandra, you haven't had –'

Cassandra again, thought Cassie, knowing only too well what was in her mother's mind. 'I haven't had a premonition,' she said. 'Sorry to disappoint you, but no spirit voices have murmured in my ear. I was just suddenly sick of Fridays and French homework and having to be up in my room without even the radio on –'

'Now, be reasonable. How can I have pop music blaring over my head? That would just about be the end. I wouldn't have a client left. Come on, love,' said Mrs Palmer, picking up Cassie's bag of school books, 'upstairs with you!'

'I don't know why I put up with it,' Cassie grumbled, allowing herself to be shepherded to the stairs. 'My friends wouldn't, I can tell you. You should hear how they talk to their mothers. They've got them just where they want them. Right under their thumbs.'

'I'm a bit too big to fit under your thumb, love,' said Mrs Palmer. 'You'll have to put on a bit of weight if you want to take me on. Up with you!'

She watched from the foot of the stairs as her daughter slowly ascended.

'I'm not a teenage rebel,' Cassie was muttering sadly. 'I'm a teenage worm. I'm spineless. I'm all soft. I'm made of plasticine.' She looked back over her shoulder. 'I ought to play my radio full volume and dance over your head. But I won't. Not me, oh no. I'll just do my bleeding homework and go to bed.'

'Goodnight. Sweet dreams,' said her mother, and turned to the dark room. Cassie, hanging over the banisters, saw her mother take a deep breath, hold it for a long moment and then let it slowly out again. Then she went into the room and shut the door behind her.

An hour later, Cassie lay in bed, her French book in her hand, her eyes fixed on the ceiling. She heard the doorbell ring once, twice, then a third and a fourth time. No more? Well, some of them would have come together. The house was silent now. Cars sighed on the wet roads, their headlights flaring briefly on the ceiling. The net curtain swelled suddenly and jerked at its wire. The French book slipped from Cassie's fingers and hit the floor with a thud. That would make them jump down below.

Now she heard her mother's voice rising, expanding to its full power in some measured incantation. Mrs Palmer, once celebrated medium, was calling the spirits out of the windy air, out of the wet ground, from the four corners of the earth, summoning them all to the small suburban house where her youngest daughter, seventh child of a seventh child, lay shivering with fright.

'Don't come!' whispered Cassie desperately, pulling the covers over her head. 'Don't listen to her! Keep away from us!'

Two

Cassie was fighting a plague of little ghosts. Like midges on a summer's evening, they swarmed thick about her head.

'Let us in! Let us in!' they whined. 'Seventh child of a seventh child, you belong to us! We need your tongue for our messages! Let us in!'

And her mother said, 'Open the door, Cassandra. Open a little wider, please.'

'Ugh! Ugh! Ugh!' Cassie grunted like a pig. She'd meant to say, 'No! No! No!' but was afraid to open her mouth, understandably wishing to keep her tongue to herself. She waved her arms, turning her head this way and that, but it was like trying to fight a hailstorm.

'I think you'd better all leave!' she shouted suddenly, in a voice quite unlike her own, and found herself sitting up in bed, all entangled with the sheets, the blankets on the floor.

Even as she looked round the familiar room for comfort, she heard the shrill buzzing continue. Not in her head any longer, but outside her door. Had her nightmare followed her out of her sleep? Were they coming for her at last, her mother's horrid ghosts?

'I said, I think you'd better all leave.' It was her mother's voice from the hall below, and she heard the noise of angry voices raised in reply. Thank God, it was only a row. She got quickly out of bed and opened the door. What had happened? Silently, on her bare feet, she walked down as far as the bend of the stairs and looked over the banisters.

Her mother was just below, standing with her back towards Cassie. Seen from this angle, with hairpins sticking out of her hair, she looked both defensive, like a hedgehog at bay, and diminished. A young man was facing her. He had reddish hair and a pale sharp face, rather like a fox. Although he was not smiling, Cassie thought he looked pleased, as if things had gone right for him and wrong for everybody else. The others, all women, stood in an untidy, muttering bunch round the hall stand, struggling into coats, pulling gloves and crumpled scarves out of pockets, and unhooking umbrellas. Cassie knew them all by sight – only the young man was new to her. He must be the nephew.

'It's people like you who bring the whole Spiritualist movement into disrepute.' It was his aunt speaking, a plump, powdery lady, with a pink and white marshmallow face quite at odds with her sour voice.

'I'm sure there must be some mistake. I'm sure dear Madame Palmer can explain . . .' but even kind Miss Curtis, who had never said a harsh word in her life, seemed unable to think of an excuse for Mrs Palmer. Things must be bad. What could have happened? What had her mother done?

'No wonder she said she got better results in the dark,' said a square woman in a brown coat.

'I've never been so taken in before,' said another woman angrily, 'I never considered you a *good* medium, Madame Palmer, but at least I thought you were honest.'

'I *was* honest,' said Mrs Palmer, 'but people expect so much. All the time. More and more. They're never satisfied. All right, I admit I dressed it up a little. What was the harm? Everyone likes to play a little joke at times. The spirits are mischievous, dear ladies,' she added unhopefully. 'They – er – they led me to –'

There was a babble of protest, from which phrases rose up to Cassie – 'Trying to blame us' – 'Joke indeed' – 'Such deceit' – 'False pretences'.

'Criminal fraud, I'd call it,' said the young man, raising his sharp voice and cutting clean through the din. 'And something ought to be done about it.'

Cassie stopped breathing and everything seemed to stand quite still. No-one moved. Then an umbrella fell to the floor with a clatter and they all came to life.

'I really must go now, my dear,' said Miss Curtis, avoiding everyone's eyes, 'I – I'll let you know about

15

next week. I may not be able to come for a time. I have so many . . .' Then she raised her head and looked unhappily at Mrs Palmer. 'Wasn't it true at all, my dear? I really thought it was Fred speaking to me. I really did. It – it is *such* a disappointment.'

'Miss Curtis,' began Mrs Palmer, but the young man interrupted her. 'Surely you'd rather *know*?' he asked Miss Curtis, and when she did not answer, he looked round at the other women who avoided his eyes. He spread his hands as if to say 'women!' or 'There's no fool like an old fool.' 'I suppose I didn't expect to be thanked, but really –.' His aunt laid her hand on his sleeve and said something in a low voice. They all began talking amongst each other. Cassie could not hear what they were saying, only that they were still angry. She crept a little nearer down the stairs.

'If you've said everything you have to say, and I hope you have,' her mother said loudly, obviously giving up any idea of re-establishing her credit, 'there's the door. It's getting late.'

'I have one more thing to say,' said the young man, turning on her, 'And it's this. I intend to take the matter further. An honest thief I could perhaps forgive, but this! Trading on the grief of silly, lonely old women! It's – it's *nasty*.' He glanced at his aunt for support, but perhaps she did not like being called a silly lonely old woman, for she turned away. 'I'm going to report you to the police –'

Cassie must have made a sound. They all looked up sharply and saw her standing half-way down the stairs, a thin child in a nightgown somewhat too large for her so that it puddled round her feet like spilled milk. (It had been her sister's, only recently handed on). She stared back at them until tears filled her eyes so that their faces wavered and broke, and only her mother's large figure stood out. Then she ran downstairs so quickly that she tripped.

'Mum!' she cried, and Mrs Palmer caught her in her arms and set her on her feet. 'Go back to bed, child.' Then, turning to the others, she said with dignity, 'Do what you must about tonight. I didn't mean any harm. If it'll make you happy to see me in prison, well, so be it. It's been a hard life, being left on my own with seven children, not that I'm trying to make excuses . . .'

They left, the women quietly, the young man, opening his mouth for some further comment, was suddenly jerked through the door and disappeared. Cassie and her mother listened to the sound of their footsteps receding down the garden path.

'Prison, Mum?' asked Cassie, frightened. What would they do? What would happen to them?

'Prison? Not on your nelly! No, of course not, you little goose. Didn't you see those women's faces before they left? What, condemn the widowed mother of an innocent child to prison – *seven* innocent children! Not them, bless 'em! Oh, it was a piece of luck you coming downstairs like that, Cass!' Catching sight of her daughter's expression, Mrs Palmer stopped, somewhat abashed. 'Now I don't want you to make too much of this, Cassie,' she said. 'Every

17

profession has its little ups and downs. And what
are you doing out of bed, I'd like to know. Without
your dressing-gown and slippers, too. You'll catch
your death –'

'And that would never do, would it, Mum. Seeing
you can't get in touch with me on the other side after
all!'

'Don't you start! Oh, what a time I've had, what
a time!' She sank down on the bottom step, pulling
Cassie down beside her. 'Cassie, you're shivering. I
wish you'd get your dressing-gown.' But she made
no effort to insist on this, merely pulled Cassie closer
to her and leaned back against the banisters.

'What happened, Mum?' Cassie asked.

'Nice cup of tea, that's what I need. In a minute,
when I've got my strength back.'

'Mum! What *happened*?'

'What happened? Everything went wrong; that's
what happened. Oh well! It was Friday the Thirteenth, after all!'

'Mum!' protested Cassie.

She's trying to think up some story, thought
Cassie angrily. And if I don't look out she'll have me
believing it, and that it was just another bad dream
of mine. Well, I won't let her get away with it.

'Mum, I was there all the time. I was on the stairs.
I heard everything they said. I know you've been
found out. I just want to know the details, Mum.'

Mrs Palmer sighed.

'Well, you're growing up. I suppose you're old
enough to know that life isn't all daisies. But don't

misunderstand, Cass . . . you kids always get the wrong idea. Like having seances in the dark. Oh I know Tom says it's because we can fake things! Don't think I haven't heard him. But it's *not*! I mean, that is, it's a temptation, of course, but it's not the *reason*, see?'

'*Some departed spirits prefer darkness*,' said Cassie, like someone repeating a lesson.

Her mother tried to judge from her face how she was taking it; but Cassie kept her face blank. 'Go on, Mum,' she said.

'You sound just like a policeman, love,' said Mrs Palmer reproachfully; and then went on:

'Well, I started off with the ruby lamp, when, all of a sudden, "*Why a red lamp?*" he asks.'

'Who, Mum?'

'That woman's slimy nephew, of course. "Why a red lamp?" "It's traditional," says I, very calm. "Oh," says he. "Why?" "*Why?*" says I; and do you know, Cassie, I couldn't remember! Of course your father could have told him, but my memory is so bad these days.'

Mrs Palmer paused. 'Why do spirits prefer a red light, Cassie?'

'Some of them might feel more at home,' suggested Cassie, pointing downwards with her thumb. 'Go on, Mum.'

She was determined to give Mrs Palmer no time for invention.

'Well, you know the routine, love. We sat in a circle with our fingers touching while I said my piece. But I knew, I *knew* nothing was going to come. I can always tell. There was no feel – no presences. Not a smell of them. It was just as if someone was telling them to keep away!'

Cassie shifted guiltily. Surely the spirits couldn't have heard her? She'd kept her head under the covers as she'd noticed that her mother always addressed the spirits in a loud voice, as if they were slightly deaf.

'It's not nice sitting there,' said Mrs Palmer plaintively, 'like a dummy with your head quite empty and everybody waiting. I had my eyes shut but all the time I could feel *him* staring. It was just like his sharp little eyes were pricking me. I ask you, love, how could I concentrate? Then, after a little while, he comes out with: "Isn't anything going to happen?" "There's a disturbing influence here," says I, still very calm. "There's an *Unbeliever*. It's upsetting the Vibrations." '

'What did he say to that?' asked Cassie. She hoped her mother had squashed him flat. She hadn't liked the look of the slimy young man one little bit.

'He sneered, Cassie. He just sneered. I could have fetched him one round the ear. Then the others suggested that we try in the dark, like we often do if nothing comes at first. "In the DARK?" says he. Oh I knew what he was thinking, all right! So I says, "We'll keep the light on, if you don't mind. If some people are Suspicious, it's best we all know where we are." '

Mrs Palmer frowned and Cassie nodded approvingly.

'He knew I meant *him*, all right. You could tell. He came over all affable. "My *dear* Madame Palmer," he says. "*Do* please put the light out if it would help. I'd *hate* to spoil the evening." So – so I put the light out.'

Mrs Palmer sighed heavily. Now we're coming to it! thought Cassie; and waited.

'It was my own fault,' said Mrs Palmer, patting down her hair as if it was beginning to stand on end. 'I should have known better. After all, it's not the first time I've dried. I should have played it quiet. And I knew it. But – but there was little Mister Know-all, sitting in the dark . . . and – and I just couldn't resist. Oh dear!'

Mrs Palmer put her hand over her mouth and started to wobble. Cassie looked at her, at first with alarm, and then with suspicion. Surely her mother couldn't be *laughing*?

'Hysterics, love,' said her mother, recovering herself. 'Just a touch of hysterics. It's been quite a strain. I need that cup of tea. I need calming down. Now, off to bed with you or you'll never get up in the morning.'

'Mum, what *happened*?'

'I've told you.'

'No you haven't!'

Mrs Palmer looked evasive. 'I'll explain in the morning,' she said.

'MUM!'

'All right then!' Mrs Palmer shouted angrily. 'All right, all right! I cheated, if you really want to know! I cheated. I used a few – well – er – props, we call them.' She looked at Cassie uneasily. 'Well, you might as well know now. Listen! Can you hear anything?'

She moved her left arm cautiously. There was a thin sound of bells. She brought her knees together. There was a sharp wooden rap.

'Not that he found *those*,' said Mrs Palmer with satisfaction.

She put her right hand into her left sleeve and produced a black ostrich feather which she brushed lightly across Cassie's astonished face.

'I never could do materializations,' said Mrs Palmer wistfully. 'Not many of us can. And that's all they seem to want nowadays. Spirit fingers,' she said, waving the black feather delicately in the air.

Her face darkened.

'He had a torch,' she said. 'The little swine had a torch. So I was caught, Cassie. Your poor mother was caught red-handed.'

That was all she would say that night, except that she was asleep on her feet and so, from the look of her, was Cassie. 'Go to bed, love. We'll talk about it in the morning!'

Cassie felt odd. She felt her eyelids drooping and her mind turning somersaults.

Mrs Palmer looked at her curiously.

'I hope you're not taking this little upset too badly, Cass . . .?'

'I'm a new person,' said Cassie. 'And I feel peculiar.'

'Cassie –'

'We'll talk about it in the morning,' said Cassie, feeling she was getting a little of her own back. 'When I start my new life.'

Three

'She'll go to prison,' said Mary tearfully, 'and we'll all have to go into Homes.'

The three youngest Palmer children were in Tom's room. They were the only ones left: the four older ones had left home long since, existing only as memories, letters and an occasional parcel at Christmas. Mary was sitting on the foot of Tom's bed and crying. Cassie was on the chair by the window, looking out into the rain. Tom was still in bed, sleepy after his late night, sipping the tea that Cassie had brought him.

'What did she say, Cass?' he asked.

'I told you. She's gone out. We just found that note propped up against the marmalade.'

Tom glanced at the note the girls had given him. It said: 'Had to go out. Back before lunch. *One* egg each. Love Mum.'

'I meant – what did she say last night? About that man going to the police?'

'She didn't seem worried. She said they wouldn't do anything. Her being a widow and all that.'

'I expect she's right.'

'She can't *know*,' said Mary. 'Not for certain.'

They were silent for a time, listening to the gas fire hissing and the rain on the window. Cassie sighed. She felt worse than she had last night. When she'd gone to bed, she'd felt almost happy. Just for a moment. She wished she could remember why.

'I hope she comes back soon,' she said.

'Perhaps she's been arrested,' said Mary, beginning to cry again.

'Oh, do stop snivelling, Mary. Or at least blow your nose! You're getting on my nerves!'

'Let her alone, Cass,' said Tom, who was soft-hearted. He took a handkerchief from the pocket of his jacket, which was on the chair by his bed, looked at it doubtfully, then deciding it was clean enough, handed it to Mary. Mary blew her nose loudly and angrily.

'Sorry. I didn't mean to be horrid, Mary,' said Cassie. 'I was upset.'

'You're not the only one who's upset –.' Mary stopped, and for the first time that morning her face brightened a little. 'You're no different from us, Cassie. What's so special about you now? If Mum's a fraud, where does that leave you? Just *ordinary*, like the rest of us. How does it feel?'

'*That's* what I was was happy about!' said Cassie, remembering. 'I thought I was a new person. That I didn't have to be frightened any more. No more nightmares! No more wondering and dreading that my "gift" would come! Recently, since I've been thirteen, I think, Mum's been watching me like a cat. As if she expected it would come any . . .' She stopped, puzzled. 'I don't understand. If Mum's a fake, if it's all bunkum, what was she expecting?'

'There's more than one reason for watching a teenage girl,' Tom said, with a shake of laughter that spilled his tea all over the sheets. Taking his handkerchief out of Mary's hands, he started mopping up.

'You oughtn't to be laughing,' said Mary reproachfully. 'Poor Mum!'

'Poor Mum indeed!' Cassie cried indignantly. 'When all these years . . . Do you know, *she* once accused *me* of cheating at snakes and ladders! And all the time – making a fool of me! Why did she do it? Frightening me out of my childish wits! How many times did I wake you up in the middle of the night, Mary, screaming *they* were after me? Mum's bleeding ghosts!'

Mary nodded sympathetically, drying her eyes on her fingers and leaving dark smudges. 'I was frightened too,' she said.

'I always told you girls it was a load of rubbish.' said Tom, yawning. 'I don't know why you believed all her junk. You *said* you didn't, Cassie.'

'I didn't when the sun shone and I was with friends,' said Cassie honestly. 'But when I was alone . . . at night . . .' She shivered. 'Oh, well, that's all over now,' she said, turning again to the window and looking out into the grey street. Somewhere in the garden below, a blackbird started its monotonous warning of danger.

'You know.' Tom's voice sounded puzzled. 'Somehow I didn't quite think she did it deliberately. Cheated, I mean. Well, I suppose I must have done, in a way, but – well, it's different to *know*.'

'Yes,' said Cassie firmly, leaning her forehead against the cool glass of the window. 'It's better! It means I'm free. I'm shedding no tears over the Other Side. One world at a time is good enough for me.'

It was a pity it was not looking its best. The rain had stopped but nothing looked the cleaner for its washing. A black cat picked its way fastidiously through the puddles, its tail pointing accusingly at the sky. A woman in a grey mackintosh, huge as an elephant, lowered her umbrella, pumped it vigorously to shake off the last drops, and looked up.

'Here's Mum come back,' said Cassie.

Seeing them in the window, their mother beamed amiably, waved, and then disappeared round the side of the house. The children made for the door.

'Hullo, dears, had a nice gossip?' Mrs Palmer inquired affably as they trailed into the kitchen. She plumped down in a chair. 'Oh, it's good to take the weight off my feet! Mary, make a cuppa when the kettle boils, there's a love. Well, I've done what I had to do,' – for a moment her large face looked a little crinkled, as if what she had had to do had taken some of the stuffing out of her; then she smiled again.

'It's all right now, my chicks. No need to worry about – er – about anything.'

'He's not going to prosecute, then?' asked Tom bluntly.

'No, no! Of course not!' Mrs Palmer said, trying to look surprised at the very idea. 'Whatever has Cassie been telling you?'

'If you hadn't gone out, you could've told them yourself.'

'All right, Cassie. No need to get upset. Now, let's all sit down comfortably. It's time we had a little talk.'

She waited until they were all settled in their chairs, with cups of tea before them, looking from one face to another and holding up a large hand when a mouth opened to speak.

'No, hear what I have to say first, loves, and then it will be your turn. Now, I do realise it's been a shock for you to find your mother has little faults, just like anybody else,' she pretended not to notice the incredulous glance Tom exchanged with Cassie. 'But as we grow older, we find the world is not black and white, like we first thought, but grey and – er –

'Green?' suggested Tom, all innocence.

Mrs Palmer looked at him sharply and snapped, 'Perhaps if you lot had been more help!' Then, controlling herself with an effort, she swallowed and started again.

'Everyone makes mistakes. We all have our little failings. Are *you* perfect, Tom? Speak up, boy, if you think you are! No? And what about you, Mary?

Never done anything wrong? Eh? And you, Cassie –?'

Her face softened as she looked at her seventh child. For an awful moment, Cassie feared her mother might make an exception for her. Mrs Palmer's blatant favouritism had caused her nothing but trouble. If it hadn't been for Tom sticking up for her, she might have found herself completely ostracised by the rest of the family.

'I'm terrible, Mum,' she said quickly. 'I own up. I confess all. I'm the worst of the lot.'

Mrs Palmer smiled and looked at them affectionately. They were good children. It was not going to be as difficult as she feared. She relaxed.

'Look, kids,' she said. 'A medium can't always get in touch with the Other Side. Stands to reason. It's not just like picking up a telephone. There are bound to be times when nothing comes. So what is she to do then? Say sorry, there's no show tonight, but kindly leave your money just the same, there's still the butcher, the baker and the candlestick maker to be paid? Mind you, that might be effective just once, but you couldn't *keep* doing it.'

She caught Cassie's eye, looked a trifle self-conscious, and went on, 'So we use a bit of – well, you might call it – er – showmanship! That's the word. Like in a circus. You know, the drums, the tinsel! All the razzmatazz before the lions come on. Well, it doesn't mean the lions aren't *real*. Now, does it? See what I mean?' She looked round at them triumphantly while they stared back amazed. 'Now, it's just the same with the Departed. They need a bit of help from time to time. I wouldn't want you to think your poor old mum was a *fake*.'

'Mum,' cried Cassie desperately, refusing to believe what she was hearing. 'Are you trying to make out that it's *true*? After last night? That it isn't all – all one big *con*?'

She felt she could not *bear* it. Not all over again. Not when she had thought she was free.

'God give me patience,' said her mother, clapping her hands together as if she wished someone's head were between them. 'Don't you kids ever *listen*? What have I been trying to tell you for the last half hour, eh? What was I trying to tell you last night, Cassie? Of course, it's true, love. I *have* special gifts, even if they haven't been around much lately. And *you*, you'll have greater gifts than mine.'

'No!' cried Cassie, in horror.

'Oh, yes, love,' said her mother fondly, completely mistaking her daughter's reaction, 'I'm not having you on. I'm only a medium, a humble passer-on of messages, as you might say. But you'll be a clairvoyant, too! Second sight! Now isn't that something? A seventh child of a seventh child, you don't see many about nowadays.'

Cassie stared at her, her face flushed. She wanted to shout out all her anger and despair at the very thought of the life her mother was laying on her again, but she knew if she risked a word, her chin would begin that humiliating wobble that precedes tears.

'Try and understand,' Mrs Palmer went on, as Cassie looked down at the table to hide her eyes. 'Try and forgive your fat old mum for being only human. Won't you?' she coaxed. 'Eh? It's been a hard life, ducks.'

Mary put her arms round her mother and hugged her. Tom muttered something inaudible. Cassie said nothing. She couldn't speak.

'Well, you have a think about it while I get lunch,' said their mother a little tartly, 'and then let that be the end of it.'

But it was not the end: it was in a way the beginning. Cassie could not forgive her mother. Having found her out, she obstinately refused to believe there was any honesty anywhere in that large body. Her brother and sister, happy that the crisis seemed to have blown over, were content to go on as before. Not Cassie. She sulked and muttered all through the weekend, calling her mother a fraud, cheat, hypocrite, liar, whenever Mrs Palmer was out of earshot, until even Tom lost patience with her and told her to lay off, and Mary said she was a liar herself.

'You believe in spirits yourself! I know you do!'

'Not any more, I don't.'

'All right then,' said Mary, 'prove it. Try and call one up. You're the gifted one, we've heard it often enough! Let's see what you can do, O seventh child! Nothing to be scared of *if* you don't believe in it. And if it doesn't work, you'll know you're normal, like us. Call one up! I dare you.'

'I don't know how,' Cassie said, 'Mum's never taught me that. You know she hasn't.'

'You've heard her. You know what she says.'

For they had sometimes crept down at night, for a dare, six of them hanging over the banisters while the chosen one, trembling and smothering giggles, had listened at the door.

'That's true. You know the patter, Cassie,' said Tom, his eyes sparkling. 'I dare you, too!'

'All right.'

'You will? Really? When, now?'

'Better wait till Mum's out,' said Mary. (Their mother was resting in her room.)

'Whom shall we call?' Cassie asked, just a trifle uneasy. 'I mean, it's not much good just calling in the dark. We have to be thinking of someone who's dead.'

'We must know *someone* who's dead. Sorry, I mean Passed Over,' said Tom.

Mary gave a little giggle. 'We don't want just anybody,' she said, 'we want someone nice.'

They sat thinking. None of them suggested their father. Cassie could hardly remember him. But from things the others had said, and the photograph on the mantelpiece of a pale man with a thin black moustache curving down on either side of his mouth, as if to leave no room for smiling, he didn't seem the sort of father to disturb if he was busy. She didn't know if their mother had ever tried calling him back. Mrs Palmer had never said.

'Didn't one of the Great-Uncles die some time back?' asked Tom.

They had many uncles of all sizes, shapes and degrees of relationship, and Cassie seemed to remember their mother saying that one of them had Passed Over.

'It was Great-Uncle Matthew,' Mary said doubtfully. 'And – and I don't think we'd want him! He had a beard, don't you remember, and it had egg on it. He was always kissing me and he smelt of tobacco.'

'Well, he wouldn't now,' said Tom, hooting with laughter. 'Graveyard earth perhaps, and worms.'

'Don't be horrid!' Mary put her hands over her ears.

Then Cassie had an inspiration. 'I know,' she said. 'I know whom I'm going to call up! Charlotte Emma Elizabeth Webb!'

Mary clapped her hands together. 'Oh yes! Oh lovely! We can't be frightened of her! Do let's have Charlotte Emma Elizabeth Webb. D'you think she'll be just as we imagined her?'

Four

There was a cemetery in the town. Part of it was new and neat, with gravelled paths, and headstones in white rows, like choirboys. There were bunches of flowers in vases, and people standing silently, their black clothes fluttering in the wind. Part of it was old and half hidden by yew hedges. Here the headstones leaned sleepily, the grass grew long and wore feathery plumes nodding in the sun, and there were only wild flowers: dandelion, and ragged robin and white trumpets of convolvulus.

In one corner of this part, where two walls met, there was a cedar tree, grown crooked with age. Its branches spread down to touch the ground, leaving a dark cave within, with a soft earthen floor, carpeted with needles. Just outside, in the sun, was a small grey headstone:

CHARLOTTE EMMA ELIZABETH WEBB

BORN 1840   DIED 1847

BELOVED DAUGHTER OF
CHARLES AND ELIZABETH
WEBB
REST IN PEACE.

They had come across it by accident. They were
walking along, going nowhere in particular, when
they saw the wall. It was a high wall, an old wall:
some of the bricks jutted out, some had half broken
away. Thick ropes of ivy hung from the top. An easy
climb, so of course they climbed it. And there it was,
their Garden of Death, as Mary called it. She had a
taste for melodrama.

Here they played for two long summers. It was
their special place and they loved it. For they'd been
brought up with the dead never properly dead but
only Passed Over, and here the dead slept so quietly;
some weighed down with heavy stone slabs, some
beneath a thick coverlet of turf, most thoroughly and
satisfactorily dead.

Sometimes they sat talking in the dark sweet-
smelling cave of cedar. Sometimes they wandered
idly among the sun-warmed graves, reading the
inscriptions and inventing stories about the long
dead. Charlotte Emma Elizabeth Webb was Mary's
favourite.

'Oh, poor little thing! Look, Cassie, only seven
years old! I'm sure she was pretty, too. Isn't it sad!'

Cassie had preferred Robert Brown (Beloved

brother of Anna Lucy Brown. Born 1795. Died 1822. R.I.P.). She called him the Poor Prisoner because his slab was enclosed by rusty railings, much bound across with bramble and ivy. Tom, who found the game childish, and usually walked behind his sisters, whistling and paying them little attention, did however condescend to make his choice: the Black Beast. His headstone was black with age, speckled and pocked with grey, and one corner angling up sharply like a crooked shoulder. It said simply: Deverill. 1720–1762. Nothing more. No rest in peace. Mary thought it must be a dog because of having only one name, but Tom pointed out that no dog would have lived so long. Cassie said he must have been poor and ugly, wicked and unloved, so that no-one was willing to pay to have him rest in peace.

They stopped going to the cemetery about a year ago. Not because they were discovered. They never met anyone: the mourners were long since dead themselves. They just grew out of it. First Tom. Mary and Cassie went once by themselves but it was sad without their brother and they bickered all the time. That was the last time they had been, but they had not forgotten.

'Shall we go tonight? It ought to be night-time. Much better,' said Tom.

'With a full moon,' said Mary, shivering with glee.

They could not remember the state of the moon, so long had it been hidden by clouds, but fortunately

Tom found it in his diary. The moon would be full on Wednesday. 'If only it doesn't rain,' he said.

But the weather had mended. Wednesday night came cold and clear, and the moon could be seen through the kitchen window, round as a crystal ball in the darkening sky.

'All right if we go to the pictures tonight, Mum?' Tom asked.

'So long as you can afford it,' said Mrs Palmer, 'Only don't go asking me for money, any of you.'

They went out into the windy streets, linking arms three abreast, every now and then swinging into an untidy diagonal to make way for a pedestrian who seemed unwilling to step into the gutter to let them by. They were glad to be out of the small, stuffy house, glad that the rain had stopped and the sharp air cooled their cheeks. Mary began to sing in a high sweet treble, only a little off pitch,

'By the light of the silvery moo-oo-oon . . .'

But the moon was no match for the sparkling streets, the lighted shop windows displaying their finery, the peacocking signs for Antonio's Bar and Jo's Fish Palace, the winking eyes of crossings and traffic lights. It was only when they came to the dark narrow roads on the outskirts of the town, where the sodium lighting gave way to old-fashioned lamp-posts whose cool circles of light never quite met across the shadows, that the moon shone out again in full splendour.

'We won't need your torch, Tom,' said Mary.

'Just as well,' he replied, switching it on and

regarding it with dissatisfaction. 'The battery's nearly run out.'

'Nervous, Cassie?' asked Mary, feeling her sister hanging back on her arm.

'No, tired out!' complained Cassie. 'We must've walked miles. Why on earth didn't we take the bus?'

'Must be economical. Mum said so,' said Tom, 'anyway it wasn't dark enough before. It's just about right now.'

'Sure you're not nervous, Cassie?' Mary asked again, feeling her sister shiver.

'No, just cold,' said Cassie. 'Wish I'd brought my gloves.'

But she *was* nervous. She'd known it the moment she'd woken up that morning and looked out of the window and felt her heart sink because it wasn't raining. She'd known it at breakfast when her mother had taken her tea cup from her and swirled the dregs round three times before upending it on the saucer. 'Let me see!' she'd demanded, but her mother had held it out of her reach, reminding her it was unlucky to tell your own fortune. 'What's it to be today?' she'd asked, trying to sound mocking rather than uneasy, as her mother had frowned at the pattern of leaves. 'Must I be careful crossing the road or will I get A for English?' 'Nothing much, love,' her mother had said slowly. 'Nothing to worry about.' Cassie had made a grab at the cup but her mother jerked it away and rinsed it under the tap. 'Just behave yourself today. Be polite. Don't go *disturbing* anyone, eh, love?'

38

Don't go disturbing anyone, especially not some-one who had been dead for well over a hundred years?

'Here we are. This is it,' said Tom, stopping. 'I think, anyway. It looks different at night, doesn't it? Yes, it must be – there's our tree, see it? Anyone about?'

The road was empty: indeed they had not passed anyone for the last ten minutes. It was not a way much frequented at night. On one side rose the high wall of the old cemetery, and on the other the railings of a park, its gates long since locked for the night. There were no houses in sight. Only the orange glow on the left, hanging low in the sky, gave away the presence of the hidden town, making it seem to be on fire.

'Ready, Cass?' asked Tom. He was shining his torch at the wall, holding it close so that its feeble light showed her the handholds.

'You might've got a new battery,' grumbled Cassie, but obediently she caught hold of a protrud-ing brick and a handful of ivy, and began to haul herself up. It did not seem as high as before: she must have grown in the past year. Soon she was sitting astride the thick cushion of ivy at the top. Looking back, she could see over the bushes of the deserted park to the distant lights of the town, and nearer at hand between two trees, the silhouette of a woman drew a curtain across a bedroom window, changing the golden rectangle to a dull red.

'Hurry up, Cass,' said Tom urgently, 'we can't hang about. Somebody might come!'

She looked down at their shadowy upturned faces, while the wind pushed at her, as if adding its entreaty to Tom's; then she turned and let herself drop into the darkness below.

Five

It was a different world into which she had fallen: the cold, dead moon was fitting queen here. Cassie, tearing herself free from the brambles that had caught her as she landed, stared round her with fearful amazement. The green tangle of leaf, insect and sun-warmed stone that she remembered had gone. All was black and silver on this winter night. Headstones, crosses and broken columns gleamed from the shadows, on and on as far as her eye could see, like the spires and chimney-pots of some weird city sunk below the earth, that might themselves be engulfed, leaving nothing but the empty moonlight, the restless dark and the wind complaining in the ivy.

'Hurry up, you two!' she called urgently, looking up at the wall behind her and longing for a friendly face to appear. She could hear quick breathing, a whisper, and then, suddenly, the sound of footsteps running, running away into the night until there was nothing left to be heard but the rush of traffic far away and the rustlings and creakings and tappings of the wind in the cemetery.

They'd gone! They'd left her. Why? Had someone come . . .? But nobody had shouted. No footsteps had clattered in pursuit. Why? Fear took hold of her body and shook it till her teeth rattled, making it difficult to think.

Was it – for a joke? Was that it? Were they now giggling together, arm in arm, on their way home?

'Beasts! Beasts!' How could they have played such a dirty trick on her? Leaving her alone in this dreadful place without even a torch to find her way home. How long had they planned it behind her back. Tom and Mary – 'I hate them! I hate them!' she wept, trying to ease the hurt with anger. Tom and Mary against her – it was wrong! It was not the natural order of things. Tom and Cassie, that's how it should be, with Mary tagging along by gracious permission. Tom and Cassie, that's how it had always been before.

'I hate them! I hate them!' she said, too hot with anger now to feel any chill, 'I'll show them!'

Her glance fell on the nearest headstone. 'I'm not frightened,' she boasted to the listening night, and walked over to the small grave. The engraved letters showed clearly against the moonlit stone: Charlotte Emma Elizabeth Webb. 'I'm not frightened.'

She would go through with it. All by herself. *She* was not a coward. *She* was not going to run away. For a moment she almost hoped she would succeed, so that she might lead a small ghost home by the hand to confound her mother and the others. She could always make something up, she thought, something so horrible that they wouldn't be able to sleep at night! That'd pay them out!

She began to gabble the words of her mother's invitation to the spirits, far too cross to be afraid of what she was doing. She came to the last words, 'Come! O, come to me! I am ready! I am waiting!' paused, and added mockingly, 'I'll give you two minutes, then I'm going home.'

There was no answer. The grass stirred and parted on the little grave, but it was only the wind.

Then a voice said, 'What do you want?'

It came from the black headstone. The one marked Deverill. It was huge. It towered above her, three times its normal height – then she saw it was a man, dressed in a black coat or cloak, so similarly flecked and speckled with grey, so harshly creased in the cold light that it might have grown from the same stone. One shoulder angled up sharply, higher than the other, but this might have been the way he was standing, leaning forward, one hand on either corner of the crooked headstone. His face was thin, the eyes hidden by the shadow of his hat, the pale skin, drained of all colour by the moon, much pocked and pitted and scarred so that the smooth, plump lips showed up in strange contrast, glistening like grey satin.

As she stared in horror, he said again, 'What do you want? What do you want with me, little girl?'

'N-nothing! Nothing! Go away!'

'But you called me,' he said softly. 'You called me and I came.'

'Not you! I didn't! Not you! I – I was calling –' Her voice failed her and she pointed. He moved out from behind the black headstone, and came slowly forward as she backed away. She was trapped, trapped between the angle of the wall and the cedar tree, that had once been their refuge and now stretched out black arms to bar her way.

He stood, looking down at the little grave, as she had done.

'So young,' he said gently. 'So young. A shame to wake her. Little things need their sleep. Let her rest in peace, the beloved –' For a moment his voice shook and his mouth twisted, as if in anger or pain. Then he turned to Cassie and said sharply, 'You didn't do it right! You've been ill-taught! A gabble of words, didn't they teach you anything? Words! Words are no good. Listen to your thoughts! The dark blood in your heart! Hear it?'

And indeed, Cassie could hear it, thundering in her ears as she stood trembling and rooted to the ground.

'Yes, look frightened, be frightened, little girl,' he went on more quietly. 'Fear is the best teacher. I learned that way. Fear and hate. I'll help you now. I can teach you . . . many things. You want to be a witch, child?'

'No!' cried Cassie desperately, then remembering her mother's warning to be polite, added, 'Thank

44

you. But I – I'm afraid I must be going. It's – it's late.'

She held up a shaking hand as if to look at her watch. His eyes gleamed in the shadow of his hat, 'Oh, your hand!', the bramble scratches showed thin and black in the moonlight, beaded with ebony drops of blood. 'You're bleeding!' he said, with such tender relish that Cassie had dodged past him and was running with the wind, before she was properly aware of having moved at all.

On and on she ran, and as in a nightmare, it seemed so slow. On and on, not knowing where she was going, blown by fear, until the laughter behind her mingled with the sound of her painful, sobbing breathing and became as one. On and on, past the tall yew hedges that divided the old part of the cemetery from the new, lurching and stumbling now on gravelled paths so that the tiny stones chattered and leapt beneath her feet. On and on, till the white headstones advanced and retreated before her tired eyes.

Once she tripped on a marble curb and fell headlong across a grave, knocking over a glass jar and feeling the dry, papery petals of everlasting flowers crumble into dust beneath her hand. She picked herself up without looking back and staggered on. How long she ran through the stone and marble wilderness, she had no idea. She was limping and clutching the pain in her side when she came at last to the tall gates of the cemetery. They were locked.

She had no breath left to cry for help. Clutching

the cold bars for support, she turned her head at last and looked behind her. Moonlight and shadows: fat shadows, thin shadows, humped shadows, tall shadows, and each shadow fidgeted in the wind. She could not see him, but neither could she be sure he was not there.

The gate was too high and too austere for climbing; no metal flourishes softened its prison bars. The walls here were of a smooth undinted brick and clean of ivy. But on the left of the gate, close by the wall, a stone angel, holding in its hand a stone scroll, lifted its blind eyes and sang soundlessly to the moon. 'I'm sorry,' whispered the frightened child, climbing up the stone arms, 'I'm sorry.' As she stood on its shoulders and flung herself on to the top of the wall, she felt the angel tilt beneath her feet, as if to take wing and fly complaining into the heavens. But when she looked back, it stood unmoving on its pedestal, its wings gravely folded at its back.

'Cassie, there you are! Where on earth have you been? I've been looking for you everywhere! Didn't you hear me calling?'

She looked down on the other side of the wall and saw her brother Tom.

Six

'One of *those*! You shouldn't have spoken to him, Cassie. You know that! Mum's always telling us,' said Tom.

Wordlessly, Cassie shook her head. He was definitely *not* one of those, if by that Tom meant one of those men in raincoats who waylaid young girls walking home through the park. He was the dark spirit of Deverill, called up in error from his grave. She hoped he had gone back to it.

They were walking back through the bright, crowded streets of the town. Cassie, hanging on to her brother's arm, looked around her with the nervous, doubting joy of an invalid who could not quite believe that all was now well. Already her experience was fading. For a last brief moment she seemed to see again the dark figure rise out of the black tombstone, the cedar tree stretch out malignant branches, the stone angel shake its mighty wings for flight; then it all vanished and there was only her brother's kind, ordinary face smiling down at her.

'You should never have been there alone,' he said reprovingly, 'not at night.'

'And whose bleeding fault was that?' Cassie demanded, when she had recovered from being speechless with indignation.

'Not ours!' said Mary.

She too was limping, so full of her own adventure that there was hardly room for Cassie's. They had run from the police! Not the entire Force but just one, who'd appeared the moment Cassie had dropped from sight over the wall, and looked down the road at the two children. Tom and Mary had promptly taken to their heels. Not even Cassie questioned the necessity for their flight. The discovery that their mother practised her profession in a manner unpleasing to the Law had unnerved them.

'He didn't chase you!' said Cassie, remembering how she had waited and listened in the shadows, and heard nothing but the noises of the night.

'We'd too good a start,' said Tom, 'He'd never have caught us.'

'Why were you so long coming back!' she asked, and they looked astonished, denying that they'd been long at all, considering how far and fast they'd run down the hill to lose themselves in a tangle of side streets, and how wearisome the climb back had been and then Cassie was not even where they had left her. Tom had had to walk up and down, calling, while Mary kept watch at the corner.

Mary was torn between the spiritual and the practical explanations of her sister's adventure, at one moment shuddering and squealing and vowing she'd never sleep again, and the next taunting Cassie for having panicked at the sight of a tramp kipping down in the cemetery.

'It's probably a favourite *haunt* of theirs!' she said, and dissolved into laughter at her own joke.

Cassie did not mind her teasing. She was too happy at being once again with her brother and sister, knowing they had not after all played a mean trick on her, and walking home through the cold, commonplace night. Perhaps their mother would have hot soup waiting, as she often did when they came home late in winter. They turned into Shakespeare Street.

'Don't tell Mum anything!' she said quickly, and Tom said, surprised, 'Of course not.'

Mrs Palmer, for all her own dubious practices, was strict with her children, and fond of saying she'd no intention of supplying bed and board to a pack of juvenile delinquents, so they'd better watch out. Climbing over cemetery walls at night, they felt, was sure to be against some bye-law or other, if nothing worse. So they drank their tomato soup, chattered innocently about the film they hadn't seen and went to bed feeling clever at having fooled their mother.

Cassie fell asleep with hardly a thought for Deverill. In spite of Tom's prosaic explanation, she still thought he was Deverill. Deverill, the Black Beast, whom she had said must be poor and ugly, so wicked and unloved that nobody had cared enough to pay to have him rest in peace.

And though she cried out in her sleep several times during the night, waking Mary, there was nothing unusual in that. Cassie was always having nightmares.

Nothing happened for five days. No policeman came knocking at the door to carry their mother off to prison. They went to school, went out with their friends, did their homework, played and quarrelled as they had always done. Cassie had almost managed to bury the memory of Deverill somewhere right at the back of her mind, though her sleep was still troubled.

On the fifth day they came back from school – to find their small garden had grown two large notice-boards. One said: FOR SALE. The other, in larger and blacker letters and with the definite suggestion that it was whether they liked it or not, said: TO BE SOLD.

Mrs Palmer was in the living-room, spreading the crimson velvet cloth over the round table, and smoothing out the creases with loving hands. She greeted her three angry children with a rather sheepish smile. They were going to move to another town, she told them. Somewhere nice, she promised hopefully, as they scowled. They were always complaining that the house was poky, the garden too small and that the trains kept them awake. She thought they'd be pleased! No, she hadn't decided where yet. She hadn't had time.

'What about school?' Tom asked coldly.

'Well, you'll have to go to a new school, won't you?'

'How do you expect us to pass our exams if we're always changing schools?'

'You're not *always* changing schools! You've been at Candel Hill for nearly three years now,' said their mother, as if it was a record, as indeed it was. It was the longest they had ever stayed in one place. They had moved five times since their father died. The reason for these moves occurred to them for the first time: Mum had been found out before.

'I'm leaving at the end of the year,' said Tom. (He was fifteen and going to be an apprentice cabinet maker.) 'It'd be silly to go to a new school for only one term.'

'I like our school,' said Mary tearfully, 'I don't want to change.'

'It's no good making a fuss, kids! I can't help it.' said their mother. She went to the cupboard and getting out the crystal ball on its black stand, placed it carefully in the middle of the table. 'I'm sorry, but we can't live on fortune telling alone.'

She stared into the crystal ball thoughtfully; then picking it up in one hand, huffed on it and began to polish it with her hanky. Cassie wondered if she'd disliked what she'd seen in it and was now trying to rub out the future.

'What about the seances?' she asked.

Mrs Palmer looked embarrassed.

'I can't go on with them in this town any longer,'

she said. 'Oh, grow up, ducks, even you must see that! Look, after the other night, I went to see the Huntley Browns and, oh well, the long and short of it is I had to promise to give up holding seances before they'd agree not to prosecute. See? The little-mindedness of some people . . .'

There was a silence. Then Cassie said, 'You mean, they only made you promise not to hold seances *here*? They didn't mind if you did it in other towns?'

Her mother looked shifty, and sighed.

'That's dishonest, Mum,' said Tom.

'A promise is a promise! You're always telling us that!' said Mary, and then, as the thought struck her, 'Oh, Mum, were you going to train Cassie to be a fake too?'

Their mother turned into a whirlwind. She rushed across the room, pulled open a drawer and snatched out a fistful of papers.

'Do you know what these are, you bleeding little prigs?' she shouted, 'Bills! Bills for your food, your clothes, the roof over your sainted little heads! Football boots and bicycles and every bloody thing you whine for! Bills! Bills! Bills!'

She threw them at her children in great handfuls, emptying the drawer. The room was filled with flying white paper, like angry albatrosses. One pecked at Cassie's ankle: she bent and picked it up. It was a postcard from Jack. On the back was a picture of a koala bear.

'D'you think I liked crawling to that bitch of a woman and her precious nephew? Not for my *own* sake, oh no! Prison would be a bleeding rest cure, I can tell you, after you lot. Ever thought what it's like to be a widow with seven children to bring up by yourself? Eh? Of course you haven't! Too busy adjusting your ruddy haloes in front of the mirror! Do you think I *like* having to cheat? Do you think I wouldn't *prefer* to keep my gift honest? You don't think at all, do you? Only of yourselves! Oh, I wish I'd packed you off into Homes, the whole rotten lot of you!'

'Mum –' began Cassie, and her mother turned on her fiercely, 'And you're as bad as the rest, Cassie,' she said, 'don't think I haven't noticed you nearly going cross-eyed trying not to see anything in the crystal ball! I'm going out now and you can count yourselves lucky if I ever come back!'

She had jerked open the door when Mary said loudly, 'Mum, Cassie saw a departed spirit on Wednesday. She did, honest! That's why we were all upset.'

In the midst of her huge whirling fury, the words still managed to catch Mrs Palmer's ear. She stood for a moment quivering in the doorway, then slowly turned round. Anger, suspicion and hope struggled visibly over her large face.

'Now what's this, Cassandra?' she asked.

Seven

Cassie was dumbfounded. Her mother didn't believe her! Or rather, did not consider that Deverill was a departed spirit at all. She'd listened carefully to all her daughter had to tell, shaking her head ponderously from time to time, and exchanging pained glances with the crystal ball. Then, when Cassie had finished, she'd said she was more inclined to Tom's point of view. Or Mary's tramp.

'But, Mum –'

'What did you say he was wearing?'

'A sort of black coat or cloak. And a hat.'

'His face?'

'The skin was rough, pock-marked and scarred. I couldn't see his eyes clearly. They were in shadow.'

'But you saw him plain?'

'Yes. The moon was shining.'

'Mm-mm-mm,' said Mrs Palmer, shutting her eyes for a moment; then she opened them and regarded her daughter wearily.

'Cassandra,' she said, 'I've been a medium for

over twenty years, trained by your dear father himself – and in all these years, with all my experience, I've never once had a materialisation. Not once! Only spirit messages for me, and I've counted that an honour. And now *you*, a little chit like you, who can't always tell a heart-line from a life-line, who hasn't even started proper training yet, you come along and claim you've raised a spirit out of the grave, fully dressed – wearing a hat, mind you! Oh, no, no, my girl! It's not as easy as all that! It takes years of experience. It's the very crown of a medium's career. Look –'

She got up from the table and went over to the bookshelf. Running her fingers over the line of books, she chose one with a black cover and gilt edges, blew the dust off it and brought it back to the table.

'Look!' she said, having found the page she wanted.

Cassie looked. She saw the photograph of a plain, middle-aged woman with her eyes shut and her mouth open, and what appeared to be a long piece of chewing-gum coming out of the latter.

'Madame Leblonde,' said Mrs Palmer reverently, 'at the height of her career.'

'What's that funny-looking stuff?' asked Tom, peering over her shoulder. 'Is she being sick?'

'Ectoplasm,' said his mother. 'That's materialisation, Cassie.' She turned another page. 'And this –'

There was a smudged, misty photograph of a girl in a white gown with a drooping hemline, wearing a band round her forehead, rather low down over the eyes like a Red Indian's only without the feather.

'Who's that?' they asked.

'A departed spirit,' said Mrs Palmer solemnly.

Cassie peered at the photograph closely. 'But she's wearing mascara!' she protested. 'Honest, Mum! Look at her eyes, that's never natural!'

'Looks straight out of a horror film to me,' said Tom.

Mrs Palmer shut the book sharply, nearly catching Cassie's finger in it. 'Of course, I'm used to being mocked in this house,' she said.

There was however no real heat left in her voice: the storm appeared to be over. If the air had not exactly been cleared by it, at least it began to smell pleasantly of eggs and bacon as their mother decided to get their tea ready instead of walking out of the house and abandoning them.

Tom shut the door softly. 'Phew!' he said, wiping his forehead.

'Well, it calmed her down, didn't it?' said Mary, when her sister accused her of being a tell-tale and a breaker of promises. 'It took her mind off all this.' – She waved her hand at the litter on the floor. They began clearing it up, stuffing the papers back any how into the drawer. 'Poor Mum, it must've been hard for her,' Mary went on, 'perhaps we are a bit mean.'

'But she usually pays cash,' said Tom, puzzled. 'How did she get all these bills?'

'They're not all bills!' said Cassie scornfully. 'Look at this, and this! And this one's a letter from Ronnie!'

She began to read it, while her brother and sister crawled over the floor, chasing the last far-flung bits of paper that had drifted under the table and behind the sofa.

'Hey, he's known about her all the time! And never even told us!' she said. 'Listen to this: "and cannot hope to continue as you are, without the risk of one day being found out and prosecuted. Believe me, Mother, I would not write to you like this, if I did not feel it my duty to warn you of the dangers of your way of life. You should think of your children. I hope *I* am sufficiently established and respected in my career, and among all who know me, to weather any disgrace you may bring upon me. It is the younger ones I'm thinking of, who have yet to make their way in the world. Think what it would mean to them to find out their mother was dishonest! Perhaps to see her dragged through the courts on – I'm afraid I must say it – a degrading and ridiculous charge. With regard to Cassie, especially, I feel I must warn you seriously that –" ' Cassie turned the page. 'Damn it, that's all there is! Where's the next page?'

She began to rummage in the drawer, scattering papers around her and undoing all their good work. Her brother and sister came to help her, entirely in sympathy with her need to read on. But it was no good. The rest of the letter was nowhere to be found.

'Never mind, Cass. He's a pompous idiot, isn't he?' said Tom, as they pushed the letters and bills

57

back into the drawer. 'He was probably going to say you'd land up in Borstal, and that's no news!'

They had never liked their oldest brother. They could not remember him as a fellow child, only as an extra, critical, much-resented adult. No-one was sorry when his firm moved him to Glasgow.

'He writes a posh letter, doesn't he?' said Mary, half admiringly. 'Poor old Mum, though. I'm on her side, aren't you, Cassie?'

'Yes . . . No . . . I don't know what I think,' said Cassie, pushing the hair back out of her eyes as if to help her see the answer more clearly. 'I'm all confused.'

Her mind felt like a ball that had been batted backwards and forwards so often that it had lost its bounce. From a tiny child, she'd believed in spirits with every thud of her heart. Then, with Tom's encouragement, she had begun only to half believe in them. Not that she'd suspected her mother of fraud, she'd thought she was honestly mistaken, like a Flat Earther. When her mother had been found out, with wooden clappers on her fat knees, and bells and feathers up her sleeves, Cassie, through all the shock and worry, had known a sense of relief. No longer would she have to try to be what her mother wanted. Her life was now her own! The whole psychic world, she felt, had been discredited. A load of old rubbish, as Tom would say.

But – she sighed. *Deverill*. He lay in her mind like a shadow, refusing to go away. Why had she ever gone to that bleeding cemetery? Was he a load of old rubbish rising out of his cold grave? Tom's pervert? Mary's tramp. Why hadn't her mother believed in him?

'I'm all muddled,' she said, depressed, 'and I can't help thinking it's Mum's fault.'

In the morning, her mood of depression was still there and she carried it to school with her. She didn't want to have to move house. She too liked her school. She had good friends there and did not want to leave them. Her best friend was a red-haired, much-freckled girl called Ann Hopper, who now linked her arm through Cassie's as they walked in the play-ground after lunch, and began planning what they would do in the Easter holidays.

'I may not be here,' said Cassie gloomily, and told her of the proposed move. She was a little comforted by her friend's dismay.

'You can't go! You just can't!' Ann kept saying. 'It's too awful! I shall have no-one left to talk to!'

Cassie smiled, though she knew it was not true. Ann was popular and there were any number of girls who would be glad to fill Cassie's place as 'best' friend.

'Perhaps no-one will want to buy the house,' she said hopefully, and immediately wild schemes of putting off prospective customers occupied their minds. Where could one buy a death-watch beetle or a woodworm? In a pet store? The topic lasted them the afternoon and earned them several reproaches for whispering in class, and still when the final bell had rung, they had not exhausted it.

'I can't ask you in,' said Ann, as they walked slowly back to her house, 'Mummy's got an occasion on tonight.'

They strolled up and down the road together, almost as if the final time for parting were already here.

'We mustn't lose touch,' said Ann, 'we must meet often. In the holidays – we can easily arrange it. And we'll write every week! Let's make a pact, Cassie.'

Cassie agreed, glad it was too dark for her friend to see she was close to tears. Because she knew it never worked that way. She had been through it all before, with best friends at previous schools, with Ronnie, Bess, Steve and Jack, her own brothers and sister, once they'd left home. She knew too well what came of such promises. At first a letter once a week, then once a month, a postcard in summer, one at Christmas and then – nothing.

'Yes, let's write,' she said sadly.

Walking home alone, after she had said goodbye to Ann, she was sunk into such a grey despair that she felt she could not bear it. Ann was as good as lost to her, and that was bad enough. Worse by far, Tom was soon to leave school – and how many miles would he run, once he got the taste of freedom? Like the others, Ronnie in Glasgow, Bess in Bristol, Steve and Jack in Australia. A fine home they had that all the children were so eager to leave and so reluctant to come back to!

Then it would be Mary's turn and Cassie would be left. Cassie and Mum, moving from one calamity to another, from one dreary house to another, on and on until they'd covered the map of England. Always waiting for Cassie's gift to turn up. And that, she thought, might well prove the worst thing of all!

So lost was she in her thoughts, walking along with her hands in her pockets, staring dully at her feet, that it was some time before she noticed that beside her own shadow, growing and shrinking as she passed under the street lamps, was another shadow, taller, darker. She started nervously and looked up to see who was walking beside her. It was Deverill!

Eight

Cassie glanced wildly up and down the street, and felt her terror fade when she saw they were by no means alone. A man and woman stood some thirty yards ahead, waiting while their poodle investigated a lamp-post. On the other side of the road, a woman dragged a small protesting child by the hand, and two youths pushed each other about the pavement in some hilarious dispute. Occasional cars and lorries lumbered by, and lighted windows shone cheerfully on every side.

Reassured, Cassie turned and examined her companion with considerable curiosity. He was wearing the same black cloak, made of a coarse, loosely woven material, flecked and speckled with grey. It was long: all that showed beneath were a pair of stained leather boots. His hair (he had discarded the hat her mother'd objected to) fell nearly to his shoulders, dark, lank and streaked with grey. He looked odd, no doubt of it. Like the leader of some lost cause, perhaps. Or an out-of-work actor. Even a tramp. Certainly he did not look as if life had treated him kindly, but on the other hand it did not look as if it had altogether abandoned him. He was not, she thought, Passed Over.

No light shone through him. His hair felt the pull of the wind, just as hers did. His tread, though light for so tall a man, squeaked faintly on the wet paving stones. She looked at his face. The pitted and scarred skin, the smooth lips were as she remembered, but now she could see his eyes. Black, cold and dull, they regarded her steadily.

Afraid again, for there was something so unnatural in his look, she said sharply, 'Go away! Go away or I'll call the police!'

'That'll be interesting,' he said, and smiled. 'If you're no better at calling them than you are at calling up spirits, who knows who may not come?'

Cassie was almost surprised into an answering smile: whatever she had expected from him, man or spirit or whatever he might be, it was not humour. But she said fiercely, 'I'll tell my Mum!' It seemed to her a far worse threat than the police.

'I should like to meet your mother,' he said politely, and then, softly, 'Why do you hate her so?'

'I don't!' she protested. 'I don't *hate* her, I'm just cross with her, that's all!'

'Anger and fear and hate are all brothers. Don't you know that child?'

Cassie wondered if he might be a mad priest, unfrocked for some nameless crime. There was something in his way of talking that reminded her of a preacher she'd once heard at an outdoor meeting.

'What's your name, Mister?' she asked, and he told her.

'Deverill.'

He must've seen it on the tombstone, she thought. It doesn't mean anything! He could've read it as easily as us, the moon was that bright! It doesn't mean it's true! So confused were her thoughts that when he asked her if she had any wax candles at home, she answered without thinking, 'Yes. Mum keeps some in the kitchen drawer. For emergencies, you know.'

The man and woman and their poodle were now approaching them. As they came beneath the lamp-light, she recognised them, though she did not know their names. They were an elderly couple who lived in Chaucer Avenue and whom she had often passed, and smiled at and said good morning to, on her way to and from school. If they see him, she thought, I'll know he's not a spirit. They can't be clairvoyant too. If they see him, I'll know he's real!

He had been talking earnestly all the while and she, only half-listening, suddenly realised something of what he'd said. Put the candles in a kettle and melt them down. Wait until they were cool, but not hardened – they must be still soft – and make a dolly, a little manikin. A cutting of hair was useful, but not essential. A hat-pin –

'What are you on about?' she demanded, shocked. 'That's witchcraft! I don't want Mum to die!'

64

'Of course you don't!' he agreed immediately, smiling at her as if the idea had never entered his head. 'Of course you don't! I was simply telling you. Knowledge is valuable in itself, whether you use it or not. Knowledge is power, child.'

Now she wondered if he were not a mad teacher, turned out in disgrace from his school and newly escaped from an asylum – If they see him, she thought, I'll know he's real!

They drew level with the elderly couple, whose eyes went first to her companion and then glanced quickly away. They had looked at him: not through him, not beyond him, but *at* him. She was the more sure of it because they had looked so quickly away again. They were kind people and wouldn't wish to embarrass him by seeming to stare at his disfigured face. Now they noticed Cassie, and smiled at her, murmuring goodnights. Deverill raised his hand to his head, as if forgetting he no longer had his hat, and bowed.

'They saw you!' said Cassie.

'Why not?'

'If you were really Deverill, they wouldn't have done.'

'Child, they're not animals! They have minds, souls, imaginations, just as you have. Why shouldn't they see me? You called me up and I am here.'

Cassie was silent, puzzled.

'You've a lot to learn,' he went on. 'Look, see that cat?' A large grey cat bulged over a low brick wall and stared with golden eyes into some deep vision of its own. Deverill raised his hand and brought it down, quick, close, no more than an inch away from the animal's nose. The cat neither blinked nor flinched. 'A mindless beast,' he said.

'He's probably blind!' said Cassie. She too lifted her hand and brought it down quickly. The cat was quicker and sunk its teeth and claws into her hand, wriggling round to bring its back legs comfortably into play.

'Let go! Let go!' she howled. 'Oh help me!' and a man came to her aid and forced the cat to release her bleeding hand. It was a stranger, short, plump, bald and wearing steel-rimmed spectacles.

'You shouldn't have teased it,' he said severely. 'Let this be a lesson to you.'

Cassie did not answer, or even thank him for his help. She was looking everywhere up and down the street. But Deverill had gone.

Nine

It was Saturday morning. Tom had been to a party the night before, returning so late that the girls had fallen asleep before he came in.

'Let the naughty boy sleep it out,' their mother had said indulgently, when she'd woken the girls for their breakfast. But no sooner had she gone out shopping than they rushed to his room to shake him awake and regale him with Cassie's latest adventure.

At first he was too sleepy or cross to understand the point of the cat.

'What's it supposed to prove?' he grumbled, trying to snuggle back under the covers. 'That cats like ghosts and don't like Cassie?'

When Cassie explained for the third time that Deverill must be a spirit because the cat, having no mind to appreciate things immaterial, hadn't been able to see him, Tom roused himself at last, muttered that he'd always known cats were sensible creatures, and gave the matter some thought.

'The cat must've been fast asleep. That's it! He woke it up and it took it out on you.'

'Cats don't sleep with their eyes open,' Cassie objected.

'Then he was too quick for it, and you weren't,' said Tom. His eyes brightened, 'We can try it out on Tiddles –'

But Cassie, her hand still covered with yesterday's sticking plaster, had no wish to make the experiment.

'Anyway, cats aren't mindless beasts. Are you, Tiddles, love?' Mary was cradling their cat, an ancient and decrepit tabby who hibernated all winter in the airing cupboard and had only come out today, fooled by the February sunlight into thinking it was already Spring. 'You've got a mind, haven't you, boofuls?' she crooned, rocking the disgruntled creature to and fro. It leapt out of her arms and walked stiffly out of the room on its way back to the airing cupboard.

'What did Mum say?' Tom asked, and when his sisters said that of course they had not told her, he immediately said, very seriously, 'Then I think you should. I don't like the sound of that man at all. He might be dangerous.'

To her surprise, Cassie could not shift him from this. In answer to all her pleadings, he replied obstinately that it was no good, he didn't like it, she was only thirteen after all, how did she think he'd feel if anything happened to her? 'He could be a murderer for all we know. He sounds mad enough!

68

Mum's got to know and if you won't tell her, then I will.'

She had never seen him like this before, so serious and so sensible. He had always been cheerfully irresponsible, ready to join in anything his sister suggested; the very last person to inform their mother of their concerns. 'For God's sake, be your age!' was a phrase often directed at but never seeming to enter his large pink ears. Now he suddenly seemed to be growing up, as the others had done before him, and she felt a sense of loss. Too many things were changing and she didn't like it.

'You sound just like Ronnie,' she accused, but instead of rising at the insult, he just shrugged his shoulders and said, 'All right. I sound like Ronnie. I don't care.'

The only concession she could get from him was that she should be allowed to tell her mother by herself, choosing her own time.

'Only don't go thinking I'll forget, because I won't. Someone's got to look after you. I'll give you till tea-time.'

'How will we know if she's really told Mum?' asked Mary, suspiciously. 'She could just *say* she had. I bet she'll wriggle out of it somehow.'

'I won't! I promise!'

'Oh, promises,' said Mary, unimpressed: she seldom kept hers. 'Why should we miss all the fun. *Why* don't you want us there when you tell her. That's what I'd like to know.'

'I'd like to know too,' said Tom. They both looked at their youngest sister coldly.

'Because I don't want you filling Mum's head with your murderers before I've had a chance to get a word in, that's why! I've *seen* Deverill. You haven't. And I know what *I* think he is. So I want Mum to have an open mind when I tell her.'

'Well,' said Tom, after a slight pause. 'At tea-time, *I* shall tell her, so if you've already told her, she'll have to sit through it twice. And if you haven't so much the worse for you!'

'I bet she doesn't!' said Mary. 'Have you told her yet that you're not going to be a medium, Cassie? Have you?'

'No. It's not the right time, *now*, when everything's gone wrong for her –'

'It's never the right time, is it? You're too soft, Cassie. You should've told her ages ago.'

It was what Tom was always saying, so Cassie was surprised when he took her side now.

'It's not so easy to tell Mum something she doesn't *want* to hear,' he said, with such feeling that Cassie wondered what it was that he had tried to tell their mother and not succeeded. Before she had time to ask, he went on, 'Mothers always want you to confide in them and yet somehow make it quite impossible. I don't know why – perhaps they can't really believe we're separate people. It's not that Mum ever refuses to listen, it's that she always thinks she knows what you are going to say and says it for you to save time. And she's always *wrong*!'

Cassie laughed, and quite forgot to ask Tom her question.

Her mother was in the kitchen, getting lunch. Cassie shut the door firmly behind her, with the feeling that if she turned to look through the keyhole, she would find Mary's eye or ear glued to the other side. Chewing-gum would come in very handy. Or a water pistol.

'Lay the table, there's a duck,' said her mother.

Cassie went to the drawer to get the cutlery. 'Mum . . .'

'Yes?'

'Mum, do gho– do departed spirits have shadows?'

'Shadows?' said Mrs Palmer, surprised. 'Why, – um –' She hesitated, not liking to admit she had no idea. None of her books had mentioned it that she could remember. 'I – I believe so, dear. After all, ectoplasm is – er – sort of material, so to speak . . .' Her voice trailed away as she busied herself with the chops.

'How do you mean?'

'I haven't time to go into that now,' said Mrs Palmer firmly, her face close to the grill which might have accounted for her flush. 'Look it up in my books if you really want to know.'

'It doesn't matter. Mum –'

'Yes? What's up, Cassie?' she said, as her daughter did not answer. 'Is something bothering you? It's your nightmares again, I suppose?'

'No,' said Cassie, and told her mother about

71

Deverill, leaving out only the part she felt might offend her.

Mrs Palmer looked worried. 'I don't like the sound of it at all,' she said, sounding very like Tom. 'Hanging around you like that! It's not nice! I've a good mind to report it to the police!'

'The *police*, Mum?'

'Yes,' said Mrs Palmer bravely, though she looked embarrassed. Then her face brightened, 'Or the teachers at school. That's a better idea! They'll know what to do!' she went on, ignoring Cassie's wail of protest. 'A man like that frightening children on their way home from school, it's not right! The school should do something! I wish *I* could see him. I'd give him a piece of my mind soon enough.'

'He said he'd like to meet you, Mum.'

'To meet *me*. Oh!' Mrs Palmer turned her face towards Cassie: this piece of information had put quite a different complexion on it. 'Well!' she said finally. 'Well! Cassie, you don't suppose he could really be a spirit, do you?'

'Why not? He said he was Deverill, and Deverill's dead. He kind of looked dead, too.'

'Well.' Her mother moved the frying pan off the gas, and sat down. 'To meet *me*,' she repeated, gazing wistfully out of the window. Cassie could easily interpret the dreams drifting across Mrs Palmer's happy face: letters to the Psychic Society, interviews with reporters, paragraphs in all the papers.

'After all, it was odd about the cat, wasn't it?' her

mother went on. 'You don't often catch a cat napping. Even old Tiddles can biff you one as quick as quick when he wants. Do you suppose he thinks I can help him?'

'Tiddles?'

But of course her mother had meant Deverill, now transformed in her mind from a suspicious character to a lost spirit in need of a good medium's help.

'I suppose you told him all about me?' she asked, and when Cassie shook her head, decided he must have heard of her from other departed spirits. After all, she must be well known on the Other Side. There was nothing like personal recommendation.

'A historical spirit!' she said with deep satisfaction. It was no wonder the poor soul talked of witchcraft, it wasn't his fault he didn't know any better. All that nonsense about making wax dollies mustn't be taken too seriously. (Cassie, who'd received the definite impression that the wax dolly in question was meant to be of her mother, wondered if she'd have been quite so broad-minded if she'd known.) They didn't have proper mediums in the Dark Ages, her mother told her, it was all mixed up with silly superstition and black magic.

'He didn't live in the Dark Ages, Mum,' Cassie interrupted. 'Much later, in the 18th century.'

'Quite dark enough, I've no doubt,' her mother said unabashed. 'Oh, Cassie, wouldn't it be exciting?'

For a long moment she was silent, lost in happy dreams of a success beyond all her expectations;

then she sighed. Foolish and ambitious she might be, but not for any dream would she risk endangering her child. Especially not her seventh child. Just when Cassie was congratulating herself that all danger of her mother's interference at school was over, Mrs Palmer said,

'Well, love, it was a nice thought when it lasted, wasn't it? But as Tom would say, feet on the ground, girl. We must be *sensible*.'

For the next week, to Cassie's utter disgust, her mother came to fetch her from school. Cassie had pleaded to be allowed to come home with Tom or Mary instead, but it was no use. Her mother said it wasn't fair to expect them to act as a nursemaid to a younger sister. They had their own friends. She kept her promise, however, and did not wait right outside the school gates but hung about a little way away, looking in a shop window and trying to be inconspicuous. She was much too large to be altogether successful in this.

'Isn't that your mother over there?' asked Ann. Cassie said hastily that they were going shopping together for some new shoes.

'There's your mother again,' said Ann, the following day.

'She wanted me to help her choose some new wallpaper.'

'I thought you were moving house!'

'To cover the damp patches,' said Cassie, glibly.

She had not told Ann *why* they were moving house – she'd been ashamed to. Disloyal, too, to give her mother away to anyone outside the family, even to Ann. Nor had she told Ann about Deverill. He also seemed a family matter. Ann might laugh. Ann certainly would laugh, not realising that Cassie's own joking about such things had been largely a sham. Now she rather regretted her lack of frankness. By the end of the week she was running out of excuses.

'You're making me a laughing stock, Mum,' she complained. 'Being brought and fetched from school like a baby. I'm thirteen! Old enough to look after myself! Anyway, he probably won't come if you're there.'

'But it's *me* he wanted to see,' said her mother, offended. However, she agreed Tom and Mary could take turns seeing Cassie home. At first they took their duties seriously but as the days passed and there was no sign of Deverill, this began to seem less and less convenient. Tom wanted to play football, Mary wanted to go to tea in one direction and Cassie in another. Finally Cassie was allowed to come home by herself, having promised on her honour to keep to the main streets and not to enter any road unless she could see at least two other people in it.

'We've frightened him off all right,' said Mrs Palmer with satisfaction, but Cassie thought deep down she was disappointed. 'I don't think you'll see him again. But if you do, you ask him back to tea!'

Ten

The next night Deverill came back. It had been a sunny day but in the evening it clouded over and a cold wind sprang up. Cassie had stayed late at school for a rehearsal of the Easter concert, and was now walking home with a headache. She had just had a quarrel with Ann. Ann, she considered, was no longer showing sufficient sorrow at the thought of parting from her best friend. In fact, Ann was already looking around for a replacement, and Cassie did not admire her choice! Not that the quarrel had been about that, of course. Cassie could not quite remember how it had started, something about a pencil, she thought. But once started it had burned with real fury, ending with Cassie's saying she was glad she was leaving at the end of the term, and Ann saying 'Good riddance!'

Cassie sighed. What did it matter? What did anything matter? Her friends, the school – she had worked hard and done well, and where had it ever got her? Was her mother pleased when she brought home a good report, as proper mothers would've been? Oh, no! Mrs Palmer hardly bothered to hide her dismay. 'Why couldn't one of the others have had the brains?' she'd been heard to mutter, eyeing her seventh child suspiciously, as if she thought Cassie were being clever just to spite her. 'Make your mind blank,' she'd say crossly, pushing Cassie down in front of the crystal ball. 'Empty your head of everything . . .' she'd hiss in her ear, as if determined to blow out the unnecessary book-learning. A medium didn't need to pass exams, she just needed to be born the seventh child of a seventh child, and that had already been arranged for her.

Cassie, however, dreamed of going to college. Sometimes it seemed as remote a dream as winning the football pools; at other times she felt if she worked hard, it might be – it just might be possible. She wanted to be a doctor.

She'd not yet told her mother this. Her mother would be bitterly disappointed. So would her grandmother. So would her great-grandmother. Not that the latter two were still alive – they had in fact died before Cassie was born. But once one started believing in departed spirits, this didn't mean as much as it ought to.

Cassie remembered, as a small child, sitting by her mother's knee, while her mother turned the pages not of a fairy story but of the Family Scrapbook. Full of faded photographs of departed Palmers, and on her mother's side, the great Torpeys, newspaper cuttings about their seances, leaflets, folded posters, letters from grateful clients . . .

Here was grandmother in a silk gown, sixth child of a seventh child, hadn't quite made it, had to take up dressmaking. Here was Aunt Rosie, Madame Lachatte as she was known in the trade, only a fifth child but she did very well for herself, until the scandal . . . And *this*, Great-grandmother Palmer, fine old lady! Had her name in letters a foot high on placards in all the towns she worked in. Much respected.

'But *you*, Cassandra,' her mother had always ended, 'you will be the best of us all! You're the first seventh child of a seventh child we've had. You'll make our name really *famous*!' And as her mother had beamed proudly, it had seemed to Cassie that all the faded eyes in the faded photographs had glared at her, forbidding her to let them down.

But she was not like them. Something must've gone wrong. Perhaps her mother had miscounted. She was an ordinary girl wanting ordinary things. She was not cut out to be a medium.

'Look what happened when I tried,' she muttered, under her breath. 'Made a right mess of it. I wish . . . I wish . . .' But she did not know what she wished and ended in another sigh.

The wind blew cold on her aching head. A piece of paper came dancing like a butterfly along the pavement and she watched her shadow reach towards it, as if trying to catch it in its windy net of hair. Then another shadow grew besides hers, not passing on but staying by her side. She knew that shadow. It was Deverill.

There were people within sight or call. No need for her heart to make such work bringing the colour back to her cheeks. She could not speak, her breath having all deserted her. He too said nothing, but watched her, as if waiting . . .

They walked side by side for a time in silence. It was not that Cassie could think of nothing to say. Who are you? *What* are you? Why have you come? the questions formed themselves in her mind only to die on her tongue. She felt he had come in answer to her half-made wish, but had she really been going to wish him back to frighten her mother? On the other hand, Tom's mad killer was hardly a more cheerful companion. She glanced at him sideways from beneath her lashes.

He was no longer looking at her but at the pavement before his feet, where their two shadows walked. His face was grave, abstracted, almost, she could have fancied, sad. He looked weary rather than tired, as if time hung so heavily on his hands that the burden absorbed all his thoughts. Had she really called him up? Was he only here because of *her*? An odd feeling, almost a protective feeling moved her. Poor creature. Poor creature, she should've let him alone.

Oddly enough, in spite of his disfigured face and crooked shoulder, she did not find him at all hideous: there was about him an air of distinction, a kind of ruined beauty that made perfection seem dull. She wondered what her mother would think of him.

'Mum says you're to come to tea.'

The words came out in a rush and she was immediately shaken by a nervous desire to giggle, for the everyday, innocent invitation sounded so incongruous that it seemed to gather to itself a sinister humour like a table napkin offered to a cannibal.

He did not smile, however. There was nothing in his face but polite acquiescence.

'Now?' he asked.

Cassie was about to agree when she remembered her mother had a palm-reading booked for tonight and the following night she herself would be out. On the point of suggesting Sunday, she hesitated, looking doubtfully at the dark figure beside her, she could not shake off the impression that Sunday was somehow unsuitable.

'M-Monday?' she suggested timidly.

He nodded. Then she saw his shoulders move in an itching shudder and all his dark glamour was gone. Fleas! she thought, edging away. Mary had been right after all, he was nothing but a flea-bitten tramp who'd been kipping down in the cemetery at nights and she'd gone and asked him to tea! She remembered uneasily how furious her mother had been when Mary had once caught nits in her hair, how she'd shouted 'disgusting' and cut off all Mary's hair and washed the stubble in foul-smelling black soap, while Mary'd wept into the plastic bowl and

Cassie'd hidden the scissors in case her own unin-habited head were no protection. Still, Mum had *told* her to ask him, she thought. Serve her right. Hope she catches them! Fleas!

Someone walked over my grave.

She looked at him sharply, not certain whether he had spoken the words or whether they had merely come into her mind for it had been indeed just that kind of compulsive shudder . . . But the cemetery was locked up at half-past five, so who could be disturbing his grave?

Worms . . . there are always the worms . . .

It was so much the sort of remark that Tom might have made that it failed to shock her. She said sharply, 'What? Did you speak, Mister?'

He turned to her immediately and, ignoring her question, said with a great air of sincerity that he admired her spirit, he liked her, she was his friend

'For *me*, no-one can ever take your place,' he said, and it was as if he knew all about Ann's disloyalty and was offering comfort where no-one had any right to know it was needed. '*I* am your friend!'

'I – I –' Her mother had brought her up too well: she could not be out-and-out rude in cold blood – and her blood was near freezing. Go to hell! I don't want your bleeding friendship! You frighten me! She was not old enough to know how to convey all this by a raised eyebrow. So she stammered and said feebly, 'Oh! Well – er – thanks!'

His smile widened a little.

81

She had stopped walking and they stood in silence. She felt she could bear his company no longer but did not know how to be rid of him. If he'd tried to attack her, she could've called out for help, there were other people in the street but he did nothing. Just stood there and stared at his shadow.

'Well, cheerio, then,' she said, and her voice squeaked like a mouse.

'Till Monday,' he said.

She'd forgotten! She'd asked him to tea! But there was something *he'd* forgotten, she hadn't given him her address! And she was not going to, either!

He smiled. 'I'll come to you, child,' he said softly, and raised his hand in a gesture of farewell. His black cloak, flying out with the sudden movement, seemed to join the leaping shadow of an evergreen in a wild dance. Then she could see him no longer.

It doesn't mean he's vanished, she told herself, he could easily be hiding in those bushes. The dark, empty mouth of the driveway did not look inviting, however, and she made no attempt to investigate. She crossed the road so that she need not pass it too closely, and hurried home.

Eleven

Mrs Palmer was depressed. It was no good telling herself things could be very much worse: sitting alone in a house nobody wanted to buy, with bills coming in and money going out like some horrible tide, she knew it only too well. If something didn't happen soon . . .

Holding her tea-cup in her hand, she began slowly moving it round so that the dregs stirred in the bottom and the big, black tea-leaves shifted. Then abruptly she put the cup back on its saucer and pushed it away from her. She dare not. Not tonight.

She sighed. I was a good medium once, she thought sadly. I used to have such lovely messages. People were grateful then – Madame Palmer, they'd say, you've been such a comfort . . . Ah, those were the days! Sitting there in my best velvet, like a queen, with all the faces turned towards me, waiting on me and the power puffing me up. What had gone wrong? She was growing old, that was the trouble. Her powers were leaving her. When did she last have a genuine message, she wondered, and could not remember. It was after all very difficult to tell which were inspired from the Other Side and which from this. She sighed again. If only their luck would change. Now if Cassie's man had really been a spirit . . .

'Mum!' cried Cassie, rushing in, her hair wild, her dark eyes glittering strangely. 'I've seen him again! He *is* a ghost. Spirit, I mean. He knew things he couldn't have known! Things I only thought! Oh, Mum, it's true!'

Perhaps because of the strength of her daughter's conviction, perhaps because she was in a mood to clutch at straws, whatever it was, Mrs Palmer listened to her daughter's tumbling words and found herself believing every one. Her seventh child had seen her first ghost!

'Oh, clever girl,' she cried, hugging Cassie till she could hardly breathe. 'My clever girl! I always knew you had it in you. A departed spirit! Coming to see me! Lord, how proud your father would've been. So young, so gifted! You'll be famous! Oh, I knew you'd have a great gift little though it showed! Let people say what they like against large families, what *I* say is, you can't have a seventh child of a seventh child without 'em! Just wait and see, I'd say, we didn't have all those children for nothing, I hope!'

By Sunday, the day before Deverill was expected, the dark room was no longer dark. Mrs Palmer had drawn back the curtains, thrown open the window, polished the tables, darned the hole in the carpet, covered the darn with a rug: and now as if she no longer had anything to hide, changed all the bulbs from 40 to 100 watts. Nor had the rest of the house escaped. Mary and Cassie were ordered to wash the paintwork in the hall, and Tom to clean the windows and trim the hedge.

'That's enough of your lip!' Mrs Palmer said, as Tom grumbled under his breath. 'Perhaps if we'd kept the house looking nicer, somebody'd want to buy it.'

After lunch, when Mrs Palmer, exhausted, went to rest on her bed, her children went into the once-dark room to admire the result of her labours.

'Doesn't it look nice?' said Mary wistfully, as they gazed round the bright and shining room. 'We could've had parties here. I wouldn't have minded asking people back . . . Oh, I do wish Mum would retire, and we could stay here!'

'Don't suppose she can afford to,' said Tom. 'And she's years away from a pension.'

'It even smells different,' said Cassie, sniffing.

'It's the flowers. Look!' Mary pointed to a vase of early daffodils and narcissi. 'Lucky Deverill! She never buys flowers for us!'

'You're not dead,' said Tom. 'You have to be dead before Mum bothers about you.' But then he laughed. 'All this for a grave-digger! Poor old Mum!'

Tom's fears had lightened with the weather. The March sun might cause the grass to grow tall and buds to swell with ambition, but on Tom it seemed

85

to have a contrary effect: he'd stopped growing up for the moment. Once more he was her happy-go-lucky brother, and Cassie's pleasure in this was so great that she was more than willing to accept his latest theory that Deverill was a grave-digger who, with macabre humour, could not resist pretending to be a ghost. Tom had explained everything. The sight of Cassie, white-faced and popping eyes, squeaking and trembling like a mouse, would've been too much of a temptation for anyone.

'I'd have done it myself,' he said. 'Yes, and given a black cloak, I could've melted into the shadows with the best of 'em, even though I'm well built.'

'Fat,' said Cassie automatically, and ducked. However, she thought a humorous grave-digger a vast improvement on a homicidal maniac. 'Though Mum will be disappointed if you're right.'

'Personally, I can't wait to see her face,' said Tom.

This pleasure was to be denied him. At supper time, Mrs Palmer placed a little pile of coins by his plate, and one beside Mary's.

'In case I forget in the morning,' she said.

'What's this for?' Tom asked, pocketing the money before she had time to change her mind.

'I'm treating you and Mary to the pictures tomorrow,' said their mother, beaming with generosity. 'There's enough there for a cuppa and a sandwich afterwards, too. No need to hurry back, dears. As long as you're in by eleven-thirty.'

Tom took the money out of his pocket and

slammed it down on the table. A fivepenny piece clattered on to the floor and rolled under the stove. Only Mary followed it with her eyes.

'I'm not going out tomorrow night, thanks, Mum,' said Tom.

'Oh, yes you are! Both you and Mary. And I don't want to see you back before eleven, is that clear?'

Tom began to argue and Mary to whine, but Mrs Palmer was firm. She was not having Tom there with his cheap sneers or Mary giggling and squeaking like a little ninny, thank you. She'd be able to deal with man or spirit without their assistance. This was her business, hers and Cassie's.

'It's always Cassie, Cassie, Cassie!' said Mary angrily.

'That's enough!' shouted Mrs Palmer, and her huge voice bounced round the little kitchen, making the saucepans chatter in alarm. 'I don't want to hear any more. That's to be the end of it.'

Cassie thought that would be the end of it. It always had been before. She was surprised to hear Tom ask in a queer tight voice. 'Are you turning me out of the house, then, Mum?'

'For tomorrow night, yes, my lad, I am.'

'Right. Right, Mum.'

'And what do you mean by that tone, may I ask?'

'I mean, Mum, that when you move from here I'm not going with you.'

Cassie stared in amazement. For a moment she had a confused but glorious idea that somehow she and Tom and Mary could stay here, while their mother practised her profession in some other town, returning at weekends . . . But then he went on talking. She realised that his plans did not include his sisters at all. Mr McTodd, the cabinet maker, had a spare room – she *hated* Mr McTodd!

'He'd be willing to have me, Mum. In fact, he said he and Mrs McTodd would be *pleased* (Now she hated Mrs McTodd as well) 'He thinks I show promise,' Tom went on happily, not noticing his sister's miserable face. 'Then I can stay at school till it's time for me to be apprenticed to him. It's a great chance for me, Mum,' already he sounded anxious, regretting that he had brought the matter up at such an ill-judged time, when he'd been waiting days for the right moment. 'He's got a good business there! I'd stand a better chance than in a big firm. He likes me and, after all, he hasn't got a son of his own.'

'Only a pretty little daughter!' said Mary. 'Don't tell me you fancy her, Tom!'

And she hated *her*, thought Cassie, close to tears.

'I see you've got it all worked out, my lad!' said Mrs Palmer. 'Your whole future planned, eh? Get your foot in the door now, marry the boss's daughter, and inherit the business later. Oh, you know which side of your bread is buttered all right! But you've forgotten one thing, my boy – who pays for the bread, eh? Who pays for the bread? As long as it's me, then I say what you do. And when I say you come with me, you come!'

Tom jumped to his feet so violently that he overturned the ketchup bottle and a little tomato

88

sauce oozed out on to the table like blood. His face was scarcely less red.

'I'm not going to! If you make me, I'll run away! And every time you have me fetched back, I'll be off again! You can't keep me locked in my room! I hate all this!' he shouted, with a sweep of his arm that seemed to include not only his mother and her profession, but his sisters too. 'It's stupid, stupid! I've always hated it! At school – the things they say! I pretend to laugh! And the neighbours peeping and whispering! I hate it all! I want to be like other people! Now I've got a chance and if you spoil it for me, I'll never forgive you!'

With that, Tom rushed out of the room and a moment later they heard the front door slam. Cassie burst into tears.

'There, love, don't take on so,' said her mother, stroking her hair. 'He'll be back. Perhaps I was a bit hard on the boy. Fancy his thinking it all out by himself! Well, he's got more sense than I thought, to give him his due. It's not such a bad idea at that.'

But that was not what Cassie was crying about. She didn't want to lose Tom. She didn't want him to marry that horrid, stuck-up Elsie McTodd. She didn't want him to grow up and forget them.

'I don't want him to go,' she said through her tears.

But Mrs Palmer was more and more inclined to consider the idea. The boy should be given his chance. If the McTodds didn't ask too much money for his keep, she might seriously think of it.

'I know you're fond of Tom, Cassie. And he's fond of you. But he has his way to make and we mustn't try to hold him back.'

'You'll still have me,' Mary reminded her. 'You won't be all by yourself.'

'You'll go next, and then I will be!'

Mrs Palmer looked hurt but said nothing. She went on stroking Cassie's hair but Cassie jerked away, jumped to her feet and rushed from the room. The house was too small for her unhappiness. If she went up to her room, Mary or her mother would follow to try and calm her down. She didn't want to be calmed down, she wanted to explode! She flung open the front door and rushed out into the night.

And the night enveloped her. It closed round her head, shutting out the stars, black and heavy and damp, a smell of wet earth in her nostrils, a bandage over her eyes.

'Why so fast, child? Isn't there time enough?' Deverill disentangled her from his cloak, and said, 'You see, I have come.'

Twelve

The front door had slammed shut behind her. She flung herself on bell and knocker: the thin ringing and the brass clamour and the drumming of her heart filled the night with the very sound of fear. Then the door opened and it was like the door opening when she was a small child crying out of a nightmare, the golden light streaming over her like a banner, the stalwart bulk of her mother standing in the doorway. She pushed past into the safety of the narrow passage.

'Cassie, what the hell –' her mother began – and stopped. Mary screamed.

'Mum, he's a day early,' said Cassie. 'It's Deverill for you.'

Mrs Palmer was silent. Cassie could not see her face, being now behind her, but for a moment she thought her mother was going to slam the door and would not have been altogether sorry. But then Mrs Palmer stepped back and let Deverill into the house.

They stared at him. Mary said, 'Oh! Oh! Oh!'

high-pitched, and her mother turned on her. 'Go to the kitchen, Mary, if you can't behave.'

To Cassie's surprise, Mary went immediately, with many a fearful backward glance, until the kitchen door shut out the sight of her frightened face.

Mrs Palmer led the way into the seance room, talking all the time in an odd hurried way, every word treading on the heels of the last.

'I'm sorry, we'll go into the parlour, must apologise, my daughter Mary, excitable girl, you know how it is, come in, come in, can I take your hat?'

'Mum, he's not wearing a hat!' said Cassie, puzzled.

Her mother blinked. She looked dazed, bewildered.

'No, no, no, of course,' she mumbled, then her voice rose shrilly, 'Where are his feet?' she cried hysterically.

'Mum!' Cassie was too amazed at her mother's strange behaviour to feel embarrassed, for where should his feet be but in his boots? 'What do you mean?'

Mrs Palmer drew her hand over her eyes.

'What? What did I say?' Then, sounding more like herself, she began to apologise. 'The light, the light dazzled me. I couldn't see properly. I'm afraid you must think . . . But it's not what I'm used to! No, it's not!'

She looked round the room, still in a bewildered way, as if she could hardly recognise it, so bright and clean and shining. Then she blinked again and seemed to recover. Drawing herself to her full height, she turned to her strange guest and looked him up and down in silence.

Cassie also looked at him, trying to see him through her mother's eyes. In the bright light from the newly washed shade, he looked shabby. There was no other word for it. The rough material of his cloak was not greasy but dull; it absorbed the light with no answering sheen but she felt if one shook it out, the air would be filled with dust. His boots were stained with a whitish mould, as if they'd been too long in water and never properly dried. His hair was lank and without lustre, his face – well, his face was ghastly enough. She was not surprised Mary'd screamed. Bright light did not suit him. He had a greyish pallor, the marred complexion pitted with shadows as if the flesh itself were half eroded. If he were not a departed spirit, he was certainly well on the way. He is sick, she thought, perhaps dying. But thin as he was, surely too solid for a spirit?

Deverill bore their scrutiny without embarrassment. Indeed, he appeared to be smiling slightly, though with the scars so near the corners of his mouth, it was difficult to be sure. She looked back at her mother.

Mrs Palmer stood, in her purple dress, nearly as tall as her tall visitor and twice as broad, her pale skin glowing with health, her dark eyes fixed on Deverill, shiny where his were dull. Cassie thought she had never looked more splendid, and waited confidently for her to speak. She would know what to say.

For a long moment Mrs Palmer was silent. Then she said suddenly, sharply, 'I'm Cassandra's mother. Madame Palmer, a medium. Do you know what that means?'

He nodded.

'Do you mind telling me who you are?'

'Deverill.'

'I see,' but it was obvious to Cassie that she didn't. 'Well, listen to me. Cassie's not a medium yet. She's too young, only thirteen. So it's no good. In our – well, nowadays, children are not allowed by law to work until they reach a certain age. Cassie's had no training yet. She can't help you. Do you understand?'

She had been speaking very loudly and slowly, as if to a foreigner, but he gave no sign of having heard.

'What are you? Tell me that, will you?'

He still did not answer but smiled.

'What's the matter with him?' she asked Cassie, in a nervous, irritable voice. 'Why won't he speak? Can he speak?'

'Yes. Yes, he can,' said Cassie, looking from one to the other, sensing that something was going wrong but unable to put her finger on it. If only her mother would stop staring with that bright, fixed eye that reminded Cassie of a rabbit she had once seen, frozen into the corner of its cage, staring at a dog.

The atmosphere of the room seemed charged with some significance that was beyond her. The light was unnaturally bright: the shadows black and still.

94

She saw everything very clearly, sharply, the very texture of wood and wool and paint seemed exaggerated until they became, by this over-emphasis, unfamiliar, unreal. And her mother just stood there, making no further attempt at conversation, but letting the silence grow and grow until the ticking of the clock was unbearable.

She's disappointed he's not a spirit, thought Cassie. That's all it is. She'll get over it in a minute. She shifted her feet and cleared her throat. The sounds were very loud but neither of them looked at her. She could bear the silence no longer.

'Are you a grave-digger?' she asked Deverill.

'Not – by trade,' he said, and she thought she saw a glint of humour in his dull eye.

'Are you – have you come from the Other Side?'

When he answered it was so softly that she was not certain what he said, something about not being able to get in, or not being allowed in. She caught the word 'outcast'.

'You're lost?' said Mrs Palmer. 'Is that what you said?'

He did not answer.

'Well, it's no good coming to my daughter for help. She's too young! She's not trained for it!' To Cassie's surprise, she made no offer to help him herself. 'So you'll just have to go elsewhere. A priest, perhaps – or –'

But whatever she'd been about to suggest was drowned by a sudden gust of wind that blew the door open and banged it against the wall, making the vases rattle. The light swung violently on its flex, the bulb crackled and flickered on and off uncertainly, but finally stayed alight. Cassie and her mother had both glanced up at it, fearing it would go out. When they looked down, Deverill had gone.

'Where is he? Where is he?' shouted Mrs Palmer, and rushed into the hall.

The front door was open – she could not remember if she had shut it properly. She ran down to the gate and looked up and down the windy street but there was no sign of him.

'What is it? Oh, what is it?' Mary came out of the kitchen, one nervous step at a time. 'What was that bang?'

'Just the door,' said Cassie, looking out into the garden. She raised her voice, 'He's gone, Mum! Come in! You'll catch cold!'

Mrs Palmer came slowly back. She did not look at the girls but walked past them into the front room. Mary followed her, saying, 'Oh Mum, I was frightened. I couldn't help screaming! He was *horrible*! Those eyes! That face! I thought I would die!'

'He's not *that* bad!' Cassie was surprised to find herself defending Deverill. 'Is he, Mum?'

Mrs Palmer sat in her wingchair, staring blankly into space. Cassie felt uneasy.

'Well, Mum?' she asked anxiously, and when her mother did not answer, said again, 'Well? What do you think? Is he a spirit? Or just a bit odd, like Tom says?'

'A *bit* odd!' said Mary. 'Why, he's – he's – Cassie,

96

you never said he was so *gruesome*! He can't be alive!
Not looking like that! Can he, Mum?'

Their mother still did not answer. Cassie saw with
amazement that she was crying. She had never seen
her mother cry before. If Mrs Palmer had wept at
her husband's death, she had wept in private: none
of her children had ever known. Now she sat, crying
quite openly, the tears running over her cheeks.

'Mum's crying,' said Mary. 'Oh, Mum!'

'What's the matter?' asked Cassie, kneeling down
beside her mother and taking her hand. 'What's up,
then?'

'I don't know, Cassie,' said Mrs Palmer, sniffing
and trying unsuccessfully to smile. 'That's the
trouble, I just don't know. I've been a medium for
over twenty years, and I can't – I can't even tell a
man from a spirit when I see one! What's the good
of going on?' Her tears fell faster, 'I've lost my gift!
I've lost my gift, Cassie! I'm no use any more! I
can't help you. I might as well give it all up.' She
turned her face away from her daughters and hid it
in her hand.

And they, who had always wanted her to give it
up, found themselves saying that of course she
mustn't – 'she was a great medium – you couldn't
expect results all the time, everybody knew that!'

'Don't let that Deverill upset you, Mum,' said
Mary.

'You told him where to get off, didn't you?' said
Cassie. 'You sent him packing all right.'

Mrs Palmer wiped her hands over her cheeks and

smiled fondly at her daughters. 'I'm an old silly, aren't I? Over-tired, I expect, and all the worry. . . . Sometimes I wish I could retire.'

'Oh *yes*!' they said together.

'Perhaps we could live in the country,' said Mary hopefully, 'and sell teas in summer.'

'A proper home,' said Cassie, her eyes shining, 'so Tom needn't go!'

Mrs Palmer looked as if she might cry again.

'We can't afford it, kids,' she said. 'What with the mortgage and having to bring the price down, we'll be lucky if we can afford a rabbit-hutch! And now there's this horrible creature of Cassie's and people will start saying the house is haunted. I don't know how we'll *ever* sell it! What are we going to do?'

That night, when Tom came home, cold and weary from having paced the streets for hours, his anger sunk to a grey gloom, he was surprised to find that the row seemed to have been quite forgotten. Mary put a cup of tea into his hands and went to pour herself another. His mother asked him how to spell 'definite' – was it with an A? – and there was no trace of resentment in her voice.

'Mum's writing to the Psychic Society,' Cassie told him. 'Asking them to send a man down to deal with Deverill. She thinks it's too serious to deal with herself.'

She stressed the word 'serious' very slightly. Tom

was glad to take the hint, and just said 'Oh,' very gravely.

He listened without comment to his sisters' account of what had happened. It didn't seem to amount to much. The man had come, done nothing, said little, and gone: what all the fuss was about, he was damned if he knew.

But all he said was, as he and Cassie were going up to their rooms, 'I wish he didn't know our address, though.'

'Mum's bolted the doors. And checked the windows. Three times.'

'I suppose I'd better start seeing you home from school again.'

'No,' said Cassie firmly. She was not going through that again. 'I'll be all right. I'm not daft. If I see him again, I'll run home to Mum so quickly he won't see me for dust.'

Tom hesitated. He didn't want another row.

'Promise?' he said, doubtfully.

'Promise.'

Tom left it at that, though he felt uneasy. A week later, when no reply had yet come from the Psychic Society, he thought of it again, and asked her, 'You haven't seen that weirdie of yours again, have you, Cass?'

Cassie had her face bent over the crystal ball. She was polishing it with a soft cloth, and seemed to be having trouble with one spot. She kept rubbing at it and did not answer right away.

'Why, no,' she said firmly, turning to look at him

straight in the eye. 'No, I haven't, Tom.'

Hidden by the duster, the fingers of her right hand were crossed. Cassie was lying. She had seen Deverill every day.

Thirteen

On Friday, he came to her again as she was walking home in the dusk. She had been expecting him.

'Look!' she said. 'Look at my knee! Liz Brown pushed me over at netball. On purpose! It was a foul!'

Deverill glanced at the dark blood on her knee but said nothing.

'Well, aren't you going to tell me how to bring her out in green boils?' He smiled, but still did not speak, watching her with his dull black eyes. 'You're not a very good devil, are you?' she teased him.

Things had changed. When she had first seen him after he had visited her mother, she had run from him, terrified, not looking over her shoulder to see if he were following, not stopping for breath until she was safe home. Panting and trembling, she had gone to look for her mother and had found Mrs Palmer sitting by herself in the seance room, her head in her hands. Although she looked up and smiled as soon as she saw Cassie, it was too late. Cassie had seen dejection in every line of that slumped figure, and pity froze her tongue. She remembered how her mother had wept, saying, 'I'm no use any more! I can't help you!' How could she tell her now?

She decided to wait for the man from the Psychic Society. She would be careful. She was not a fool. Surely she could manage for a little while without running for help. She told no-one: not Tom, who was going to leave them for the McTodds, not Mary who would be sure to tell their mother, not Ann. If Ann Hopper no longer wanted to walk home with her, preferring the company of Liz Brown, well then, she was welcome to her. Liz Brown who was rich and never wore grubby plimsolls like Cassie, or had holes in her jumpers like Cassie, and who would still be here next term unlike Cassie!

She had another companion now. She did not have to walk home alone. Not a very impressive one, perhaps, certainly Liz Brown would wrinkle her pink snout at him (he was such a shabby ghost) but one who appeared to like her company, else why did he keep coming? As the days passed she became accustomed to being haunted, and no longer trembled and turned white when she saw him. When he did not come, she was almost disappointed and lingered through the darkening streets, as if waiting for him.

That he was some sort of evil spirit she could not doubt, but his temptations struck her as so absurd that she could not take them seriously. She did not want Jack Bryde's dog to die because Jack had pulled her hair. Or Mr Croft to be stricken with stomach cramps because he had given her a bad mark for her essay. He seemed to know whenever she was cross and would start telling her some absurd recipe for revenge. One night it had been a method of bringing a victim out in purulent green boils, and that had been too much for Cassie. She'd laughed aloud.

When he'd turned to look at her, she'd felt suddenly anxious.

'I haven't any enemies,' she'd protested quickly. 'I don't want to know any of that. You won't – you won't do anything by yourself, will you?' He shook his head. 'Only if you do, I'd – I'd have you put down. Laid. Exorcised.'

Something stirred in his dark eyes, and he'd said softly that he would have to be careful. She'd frightened him there! That was good! That'd keep him in order!

'I don't want anyone hurt, see? I can look after myself. We don't do things your way any more.'

He'd nodded, almost humbly, and said that he only wanted to serve. Odd how he seemed to defer to her. As if she was someone important. Nice. Nobody else had ever seemed particularly impressed by her. Even her mother was disappointed her gift was so long in coming. Yes, it *was* nice to be treated with respect, even by a ghost. Perhaps she would be a great medium one day. Perhaps it wouldn't be so bad . . .

She day-dreamed. Madame Cassandra in a velvet gown. Long black hair held back by a silver comb.

High up on a platform in a crowded hall. Posters outside and her name in letters six foot high (see that, Great-grandmother Palmer!) Summoning, with her pale hands upraised, anyone she chose. All history to choose from – those who wanted privacy would have to stay alive! Scholars would come from all over the world to consult her. 'Actually the Battle of Hastings was 1067, not 1066. It was wrongly recorded by a scribe's error. William himself told me only last night . . .

Then she'd laughed at herself. If other spirits told her as little as Deverill had done, she wouldn't get far. Often she'd asked him what he had been, what sort of man, when he was alive. Sometimes he would say it had all been so long ago, how could he remember something so brief and unimportant? Sometimes he would quote her own careless words in the cemetery. 'Poor and ugly, wicked and unloved', but with a smile as if to show he bore no grudge. Mostly he just did not answer.

She looked at him now, as he walked beside her. He must have been a warlock or something like that. He was always trying to teach her spells and curses. Perhaps his mother'd been a witch, and taught him. 'Fear is the best teacher' he'd said in the cemetery. 'Fear and hate.' She can't have been kind. Perhaps she beat him every time he forgot. Perhaps she'd been burned – did they still burn witches in the eighteenth century? Or were they hanged?

She glanced at him briefly. Grey as his face was, it didn't look charred, but the collar of his cloak came right up to his chin and might easily conceal scars. She felt sure he must have come to a bad end, one way or another. There was a ducking test they used to put witches to, she remembered: if they sank and drowned, they were innocent, but if they stayed afloat, then they were guilty and hanged for it.

'It's not very fair!' she said indignantly.

'What is not fair?'

'Oh, nothing.' Should she ask him? 'Are you afraid of fire?' she asked.

'No.'

He can't have been burned then. Nor been in Hell, come to that. Where had he been?

'You never tell me anything,' she grumbled mildly. 'You never answer my questions properly.'

Usually he ignored such complaints, but now he asked her what she wanted to know.

'Where do you go when you're not with me?'

'Nowhere. There's no time when I'm not with you.'

'You mean you're always there? Even when I can't see you?' she asked, alarmed and a little shocked at the thought.

But he shook his head and said something she could not understand about time, something about different rhythms. Seeing her look puzzled, he added that what was a lifetime to one, was to another the blink of an eye.

'Oh,' she said doubtfully. 'You just blink your eye, and meanwhile I've been home, gone to bed, got up, gone to school, and there I am as if I'd never

105

been gone?' He nodded. 'Then since you died, all those hundreds of years until I called you up, nothing happened? You didn't go to – (She had been going to say Hell, but it seemed tactless.) 'You were just sort of sleeping?' He said nothing. 'It must make eternity seem very short,' she said after consideration.

'No!' he cried, with terrible anguish. 'I had bad dreams!'

'Oh! Poor Mr Deverill!' Cassie was moved to pity: she thought she knew all about bad dreams. She put out her hand to touch his arm: her fingers seemed to stop of their own accord just before they reached him. 'I'm sorry, sorry,' she repeated, wishing to comfort him and not knowing how.

'But it is over now,' he said, smiling at her. 'You are my friend.'

She looked away guiltily, remembering the man from the Psychic Society who would be coming to deal with him. What would they do to him? she wondered for the first time. Would he be exorcised? Sent back to his nightmares in the dark? Would he be kept for investigations, experiments, bits cut from his finger nails, his hair, his skin for analysis? And how would they keep a spirit? Well, they would have to catch him first.

And she would have to help them! It was no good – she could not have him haunting her for the rest of her life. It was too – too peculiar. She could put up with it now because she knew it was only for a short time. It wasn't her fault, she thought angrily, trying to rid herself of the sour taste of betrayal, she hadn't asked him to be her friend. He would have to go!

'How can I serve you?' he asked, watching her. She hoped uneasily that he could not read her thoughts.

'Not by teaching me witchcraft!' she said irritably. 'It's silly!'

'What do you want?'

'Oh, I don't know!' She looked at the grey, dusty street and her new dreams of being a famous medium no longer seemed attractive. 'I want a house in the country, well, perhaps on the edge of town. With a shop, a small shop, tobacco and sweets, that sort of thing, that Mum could manage if she retired. It must have a large garden for Mary's Teas, with a tree for climbing, oh, and with a river running at the bottom with a boat for Tom. And none of the rooms must be dark it must be all sunlight, and, and near enough for us to go to the same school.'

She ran out of breath and looked to see how he was taking her extravagant request, but he had gone. She shrugged. She was used to his sudden comings and goings and no longer looked up and down the street to see where he might be hiding.

'Ask him for anything useful,' she muttered. 'That's the way to get rid of him.'

Her tea was on the table when she got home. Tom and Mary had already had theirs and gone out again, but her mother sat beside her to keep her company.

'Cassie,' said Mrs Palmer, and then again, more loudly, 'Cassie!'

'Mmm?'

'Have you seen that – that creature again?'

Cassie tried to look innocent. 'No, Mum.'

'Oh dear! Not that I want you to, I'm sure! But – Cassie, I'm talking to you!'

'What?'

'I wish you'd listen to me sometimes. You always seem to be in a dream recently. I've had a letter from the Psychic Society. They're sending someone round to see us on Tuesday evening. A Mr Roberts. Now she had her daughter's full attention. 'Perhaps I was a bit hasty sending that letter. It'll look a bit silly. I mean, as he hasn't been back.'

Cassie said nothing. She was wondering whether to tell her mother now and if so, how to begin, when her mother went on.

'Do you think he'd come if we had a seance? You wouldn't have to do anything, love, only be there – you see, you might be a sort of cataract.'

'Catalyst,' corrected Cassie absently. 'Mum, what will happen to him?'

'Who?'

'Deverill.'

'Well, um –' her mother began, looking a little baffled. 'Well, he wasn't very nice, was he? So I suppose they'll just send him back where he came from.'

'Supposing he doesn't want to go? Supposing he was unhappy there?'

'Then he should've thought of that sooner. It's a bit late now,' said her mother heartlessly. 'I'm sure it's a lesson to all of us.' Seeing her daughter look sad, she patted her arm and said tenderly, 'You've been worried, haven't you pet? I've noticed. Never mind, it's nearly over now. I'll tell you what, if it's fine we'll go out for the day on Sunday. That'll cheer us up.'

Poor creature, thought Cassie sadly. Poor old Deverill.

Fourteen

'It's not my idea of a day out!' said Mary.

'But it's lovely out there, right on the edge of the town. Almost in the country, isn't it, Tom? You might even see cows.' Mrs Palmer had once stayed at a dairy farm as a child and had never forgotten it.

'Oh, cows! Oh, how can we wait?' said Mary, clapping her hands and assuming a face of such exaggerated delight that Cassie laughed.

It was Sunday and they were going to see the McTodds. At least, Tom and Mrs Palmer were going to see the McTodds to discuss his staying there when the Palmers moved; while Mary and Cassie were to enjoy the delights of the almost-country air. Then they would all have tea together, 'somewhere nice', Mrs Palmer promised.

Tom sat next to Cassie on the bus, pushing past Mary to do so, and when the bus started, hissed in her ear,

'You know it's very childish to sulk.'

'I'm not sulking,' she said, surprised.

'Damn it all, I'll be coming home every weekend, – wherever home may be by then. I'm not exactly going to the moon!'

'Oh, *that*! Suit yourself, Tom,' she said, staring absently out of the window, 'I don't mind any more.'

Tom muttered furiously under his breath but Cassie did not hear him. Staring out of the window, she did not see the rows of little houses streaming past, the men polishing their cars till they winked at the sun, the children with their tricycles and skipping ropes, shrill as birds; she saw instead a grave in the old cemetery, a grave with a black headstone. A cold moon shone and the night wind tugged and scratched at the long grass, disturbing the sleeper below. Bad dreams . . .

'But it's not my fault!' she muttered.

'I suppose it's mine!' said Tom angrily. 'Shall I tell them I've changed my mind, then! Shall I? Well, shall I, Cass? Is that what you want?'

'What?'

'All right! You win! I'll tell Mum I don't want to go after all. To hell with everything!'

The misery in his voice at last penetrated Cassie's absorption and she spent the rest of the journey reassuring him. This proved so difficult that she began to wonder if he had not got cold feet now that the time was drawing near. They had had an offer for the house at last. Not a very good offer, but one they were not in a position to sneeze at, their mother said. Now all that remained was to find somewhere they could go.

'Lucky Tom,' said Mary enviously, as they left their brother and Mrs Palmer at the McTodds, with instructions to come back in an hour when the business should be done, and Mrs Palmer obviously hoped they would all be invited to stay to tea. 'It *is* nice out here, isn't it? Look, there actually are some cows in that field! I suppose we'll have to go and look at them or Mum will never forgive us.'

In spite of the sun, there was a cold wind blowing and the two girls soon got tired of admiring the cows, who, gazing at the proffered handfuls of grass with disinterest, turned their backs and drifted off to the other side of the field.

'Mindless beasts,' said Cassie.

'I'm cold,' complained Mary. 'Let's go and see if there's anywhere we can have tea.'

It was then they found the house. It was a pretty house, freshly painted white, its windows bright in the sun. There were snowdrops in the grass and an almond tree in blossom. Neither too big nor too small, it looked as if it had grown rather than been built, so comfortably did it sit among its trees.

'Why, it's a sweet shop!' said Mary, 'I've never seen a shop with a front garden before, have you? Let's buy some chocolate.'

'It's for sale,' said Cassie, pointing to the notice board, an odd expression on her face, 'and look, it says Teas back there! I expect there's a river at the bottom of the garden, and a tree for climbing.'

'How did you know?' asked Mary curiously. The old lady, who'd sold them two bars of chocolate and kindly made them some tea, even though, as she explained, she wasn't really doing Teas any more, let them take it out into the back garden. It was a large garden, much bigger than one would have expected from the front, and somewhat overgrown.

'It got to be too much for me,' the old lady said, as if ashamed of it. There were wooden benches and iron chairs and tables, once painted white, scattered over the grass. 'We did a brisk business in the summer,' said the old lady, looking sadly at the rust, 'people come for the river. There's boating at Greenstone Bridge. You mustn't go by this,' she said, apologising for the gleaming strip of water at the bottom of the garden, that soon lost itself in a mysterious tunnel of willow, the half-rotted landing stage, the water-logged punt tied to a post, at all of which the children gazed with longing and delight, 'This is only a small tributary. You want to go to Greenstone Bridge for the boating.'

'Tom could soon mend that,' said Cassie, looking at the punt, 'and Mary and I can paint the table and chairs . . .'

The old woman laughed and said they'd better start saving their pocket money if they wanted to buy the place.

'You'll have to be quick, though,' she added jokingly, 'it's a good property. It won't be long on the market.'

'We're looking for somewhere,' Cassie told her with dignity, 'I think we'll tell our mother about this. It might possibly suit.'

'Oh, Cassie!' said Mary, her eyes shining. 'D'you really think? —'

'It needs a lot done, of course,' said Cassie, who was not without business sense. Then she asked the price and the old lady, although still not taking the children seriously, told her.

'I'm sorry, kids,' said Mrs Palmer on the bus going home, 'But we just can't afford it. Oh, it's a nice place all right. I'm not saying I wouldn't like it too! But it's too expensive. It'd take an extra two thousand, if not more, and where's that going to come from. I'm mortgaged up to the hilt already.'

Her children suggested she could borrow it.

'Borrow it! I don't mix with High Society, you know! I'm not on visiting terms with millionaires! And if you're thinking of your brothers or Bess, forget it! It's me what has to shell out there! Our family aren't exactly on top of the tree. If I could borrow a tenner, I'd be surprised. And delighted, believe me.'

Tom suggested the Bank but his mother said it took all her courage to sidle into the bank sideways, let alone be foolish enough to ask to see the manager. 'It's no good, loves. I'm sorry, but there it is.'

Cassie could not believe it. It was her house, she knew it was. It was the house she had asked Deverill for, in every particular. She had expected the price would be right to the last penny, exactly what they were getting for Number Eleven, Shakespeare Street.

'What's the good of a house we can't afford?' she stormed at Deverill on Monday evening. She had been dawdling in the streets for what seemed like hours, waiting for him, afraid he was not going to come just when she wanted him. When at last she saw his shadow next to hers on the pavement, she was chilled to the bone, and exceedingly cross. 'Don't try to look as if you don't know anything about it!' though his expression had not changed. 'It can't be a coincidence!'

Even as she said it, her reason puzzled that it could be anything else. Deverill hadn't built the house, it wasn't that old. Deverill hadn't fixed the price. What could it have to do with him? Except 'What do you want?' he'd asked, and out of her longing for a proper home where they could all be together, she'd idly described a house that she had never seen . . .

'What do you want?' he asked again, watching her, 'Money? Is that all, child? I know of a hidden treasure –'

'As it happens, you know of a hidden treasure!' said Cassie scornfully. 'How convenient! The Crown Jewels, perhaps?'

He smiled and shook his head, 'I used to live in this town,' he looked round at the dingy street, the dustbins and boxes of rubbish waiting for tomorrow's collection, the tawdry shops. 'It was different then. This was grass where we are walking. Grass and buttercups and meadowsweet. There was a great oak tree, I remember . . .' He looked round once again and shrugged. 'It was a long time ago.'

Cassie found it difficult to imagine him alive, walking through the meadow in the sunshine.

'Were you a farmer?' she asked.

'No. No, this was not my meadow. My house is further on. It still stands. I've seen it. We passed it together, you and I, one night. But you did not look at it.'

'Where?'

'I could take you there. Now, if you like.'

'I'm not supposed to go off with strangers,' said Cassie suspiciously, and he made no effort to persuade her, merely smiled and shrugged.

They walked on in silence. 'Whose treasure was it?' she asked, for the thought of buried treasure could not altogether be resisted.

'Mine,' he said, and told her he had hidden it in the house himself from thieves and enemies. In the attic, underneath the dormer window, a loose floor board, a metal box, 'Gold mostly, a little silver, a small pearl brooch.' They might have been pebbles from the boredom in his voice as he described them. 'They are no use to me now,' he said, smiling at her, 'I give them to you. They are yours if you want them.'

'In return for my soul, I suppose,' said Cassie coldly, 'I'm not stupid, Mr Deverill! I know all about devils and how they go about these matters.'

She heard him laugh: there was both amusement and exasperation in the sound.

116

'I don't want your soul,' he said, 'such a little one, what should I do with it? It would be lost in my pockets. And I am not a collector of souls.'

'What are you then?' she challenged him, and he turned his head away and became silent. Down Milton Street, Spenser Street, left into Marlowe Drive – Cassie's steps became slower.

'Is it far from here?' she asked.

'No.'

'I suppose there's no harm in just looking at the house,' she decided.

Fifteen

It was a narrow street that was vaguely familiar, although Cassie could not remember when she had been there before. On one side were warehouses, shut and padlocked. On the other, a few brick villas, an empty shop with cracked and white-washed windows, a chapel, some more villas.

'There!' said Deverill, stopping and pointing across the street, 'The one with the grey door.'

Cassie's first thought was that if he had been wicked, he had not profited by it. She didn't know what she had expected. A mansion, perhaps, behind a high, unfriendly wall. Or a house striped with dark beams, with leaded windows and a post for hitching horses. Even a thatched cottage, anything but this! Here was no fitting residence for hidden treasure.

It was the middle house in the middle of a terrace of five houses, tall, thin, shabby and unremarkable. They had no front gardens but rose straight from the pavement. Although straight was the wrong word, rather they leaned upon each other, as if weary with the weight of years, and suspicious of their brash new neighbours. She thought whoever built them must've been tired, or worried, or even in love, so little had he kept his mind on what he was doing. The front doors were so low that even a man of average height must stoop to enter. The windows were of different shapes and sizes, even the roofs humped up and down like a caterpillar. It was difficult to find anything polite to say about them.

'I expect they were quite smart when they were new,' she ventured.

Deverill did not answer and she glanced at him. He was staring across the road, his face in shadow so that it was difficult to read his expression. She thought the corner of his mouth quivered, but whether with amusement or grief, she could not tell. She looked back at the house. A light shone from the ground floor window.

'Who lives there now?' she asked.

'An old woman,' he said softly, not taking his eyes from the house. 'Old and lame and deaf and nearly blind.

'Poor thing!' said Cassie sharply.

'Poor thing,' he agreed gravely.

'What are you going to do?' she asked. 'Knock on the door and ask if you can claim your treasure?'

'I?' he asked in surprise, 'I can do nothing. The treasure is there. You must take it if you want it.'

'Why me? Why not you?'

'Because I cannot,' he met her suspicious stare with his blandest smile. 'Remember the cat, child?

I did not exist for it, it had no soul to know me. Nor would I exist for that door. It would not recognise my touch. It would not feel my finger on the latch. Besides,' he added more practically, 'it is locked.'

'So you expect *me* to do it for you? Knock, knock! Who's there? Cassie Palmer, ma'am. I left some treasure in your attic, may I go and get it? She's probably lived there since long before I was born!' He was silent. 'Or do you expect me to steal it? Is that it? Oh, you're a cunning old devil!' she said bitterly.

'You must do what you want, child,' he said calmly. As he spoke, the light in the window went out, and a few minutes later, the front door opened. A small, bent woman came out, with a fat pug on a lead. She slammed the front door behind her, fumbled with a key, locked it, tested it to see it was properly shut; and then shambled down the street very slowly, stopping every now and then to let her pug enjoy the various smells.

'She has a dog,' said Cassie.

'The dog too is old and deaf and nearly blind – poor thing,' he added, with a sidelong smile at Cassie.

'I'm not a thief,' she said.

'Of course not,' he agreed.

'Was the treasure really yours?'

'Yes.'

'Why should I believe you?'

'I can think of no reason,' he said, bored.

They were silent. The old woman was still only half-way down the street.

'She locked the door. I couldn't get in even if I wanted to. Which I don't.'

There was a narrow way at the back, between high walls, he told her, leading to the gardens of all five houses.

'She'll have locked the back door too.'

He shrugged, seeming to have lost interest. She looked up at the top window in the attic, below the window, a loose floor board, a metal box . . . Gold mostly, a little silver, a small pearl brooch. Suddenly she laughed.

'I don't think an estate agent would accept it. They like proper money nowadays.' He smiled but did not answer. 'And I couldn't sell it! I mean, they'd want to know where I got it.'

But even as she said it, she saw a way round the difficulty. *Buried* treasure, buried in the garden of Number Eleven, Shakespeare Street on Monday, discovered on Tuesday, sold on Wednesday, no, it was not as simple as that!

'It would still be stealing,' she said regretfully, 'even if it was really yours once. You can't possess anything when you're dead, can you?'

'I had no child,' he said, 'I give it to you.'

'I think it belongs to the Crown,' she said, 'at least, you have to give up most of it . . .'

There might still be enough, even if they gave the Crown their cut. It didn't belong to the old lady, did it? Just because it was in her house? It had been

Deverill's and Deverill said it was now hers. Morally – but at that word, she stopped and frowned.

'What do you want from me?' she asked, 'what do you want for the treasure?'

'Nothing. Nothing at all. There is no bargain. You are my friend.'

She thought again of the man from the Psychic Society who was to come tomorrow, and it seemed to her there was a bargain. It was no act of a friend to betray.

'I can't do it,' she said, but whether she meant she could not take his treasure or could not betray him, she did not know. She looked towards him: he was gone and there was no-one in the street but the old lady just disappearing from sight round the corner, pulling her little dog after her.

Cassie stood shivering in the wind and staring at the house. It fascinated her. She knew she ought to go home and do her homework, but she could not leave. Her eyes returned again and again to the window at the top of the house. She thought of the little shop in the sun, with the river at the bottom of the garden. She thought of her mother sitting with her face buried in her hands. She thought of the bills drifting on to the doormat, and the way her mother stuffed them into the drawer and slammed it shut. She thought of Tom's going to live with the McTodds and being afraid he might not like it.

And as she thought of all this, she began to walk, slowly at first and then more quickly, until she was almost running. She found herself in a narrow way between high brick walls, counting the garden doors – one, two, three . . . She stopped, hesitated – and then opened the door. It led into a narrow, dishevelled garden. The long grass clung to her ankles, briars caught at her clothes, but she went forward. The backs of the houses were dark. No lights showed at the windows. She stood with her hand on the handle of the back door, listening to the sound of her heart. Then she turned the handle and pushed.

The door opened. She was in a kitchen. There was very little light but she could just make out the shape of a kitchen table, with a milk bottle on it and a loaf of bread, a sink, a gas stove – there was something on the gas stove, oblong and small. She picked it up and shook it. A box of matches.

It seemed like an omen. The hall was so dark. The light switch evaded her searching fingers. She would never have found her way but for the matches. The stairs were of wood, uncarpeted, her footsteps clattered on them, but no-one challenged her. Match after match flared and flickered in the dark, and the shielding fingers glowed red. Up and up, it seemed endless, but at last she reached the top.

She stood, panting, gazing at the attic door till the match singed her fingers and she blew it out. Then she sat on the top step in the dark and knew she could not do it. She seemed to see herself, tin box of treasure under her arm, creeping down the stairs, and there was an old lady standing in her way, staring at her with pale bewildered eyes, so old and frail and feeble that a touch would send her tumbling to the bottom to lie still. A kick would do for the little fat dog, and Cassie could run and get clean away. No-one would ever suspect her. No-one would ever know. Except Cassie herself.

And then, at night, the old lady would once more tumble down the stairs, over and over again, every night as long as she lived, falling and falling . . . And when she was dead – 'I have bad dreams,' Deverill had said. She shivered. It wasn't worth it! It just wasn't worth it, she thought, and striking another match with trembling fingers, walked down the stairs and out of the house, through the back garden and out into the street once more. Standing with the wind in her face, she breathed again.

'He is a devil, he really is!' she said to herself as she hurried home, 'and tomorrow night, I'll betray him with pleasure.'

Sixteen

Tuesday morning. At breakfast Cassie decided to make her confession.

'Mum,' she said, 'don't be cross but I'm being haunted.' And she told them everything, even about going into the old lady's house after the treasure. It did not seem to go down well with toast and marmalade. They all stared at her, and their faces did not look friendly.

'I thought I'd better tell you before Mr Roberts came,' she said weakly.

'You should've told me before,' her mother said, looking hurt and worried, 'I'm your mother. You should've told me.' Then she sighed, looked at her daughter, opened her mouth, then shook her head and sighed again.

'Thank God Mr Roberts is coming tonight,' she said finally.

Tom said nothing. He had given Cassie one long stare and then looked down at his plate, avoiding her eye. Not because he was trying to keep a straight face, she thought, for he looked nowhere near laughter. After a moment, he made an excuse to leave the table, saying he wanted to be at school early.

Only Mary was sympathetic. She linked her arm through Cassie's as they walked to school and wanted to know every detail, what had he said to her, what had she said to him, could she see through him?

'What's up with Tom?' Cassie asked, when they parted. 'He seemed a bit off!'

'He thinks you're mad,' said Mary, not from spite but simply because she could never keep things to herself. 'He was saying you ought to see a psychiatrist.' Seeing the hurt look on Cassie's face, she blundered on, making things worse. 'It's Ronnie, really. Remember the letter we read? The one to Mum saying he was worried about you? Well, we found the other half. It said if Mum kept filling your head with all her nonsense, he feared for your sanity.'

'Oh thanks,' said Cassie bitterly. 'Thanks very much for those kind words!'

She had been going to ask Tom a favour. She'd be damned if she would now!

'Mary, what are you doing after school?'

'I'm going to the pictures with Betty. Why?'

'It doesn't matter. I just wondered,' said Cassie. She had wanted a companion for the journey home. There was always Ann.

Tuesday afternoon, at ten-past four, Cassie started

walking home alone. She had asked Ann to walk with her, and Ann had refused. Ann was going to tea with Liz Brown. Cassie had then asked all the other girls in turn, without success. Was everyone going to tea with Liz Brown?

'She asked you too, Cassie,' said Ann. 'Don't you remember? It's her birthday. You said you had to see a man about a dog. She thought it awfully rude, you know.'

'Sorry,' muttered Cassie. It *was* rude: Deverill, whatever he might be, was not a dog.

Now what was she going to do? Walk home very quickly. Walk home another way. And above all, if she did meet him, she must not let him know she was going to betray him. Deverill was an uncomfortable friend; what would he be like as an enemy? Once she was home, she would be safe. Mr Roberts, with the whole of the Psychic Society behind him, would know how to protect her. Until then, she had better keep Mr Roberts right out of her mind. She began to walk very quickly.

It was in Milton Street that Deverill came to her. When she saw out of the corner of her eye the dark figure beside her, she started reciting softly under her breath:

' "Full fathom five thy father lies, Of his bones are coral made; Those are pearls that were" – pearls that – pearls . . . I didn't take your treasure,' she said.

'It is not at the bottom of the sea,' said Deverill. 'Nor had it anything to do with my father.' He did not smile. His dull black eyes looked sad, as if he already knew she intended to betray him.

'I can't talk tonight,' she said quickly, 'got to revise for an English test. Sorry.' But every verse she'd ever learned by heart seemed to have deserted her. 'Nothing of him – nothing that doth fade – nothing – It was no good. All the words flew out of her mind: there was only Mr Roberts left.

'What? What are you going to do?' asked Deverill, his voice sharp.

The thought of Mr Roberts of the Psychic Society was now so large in her mind that she felt it must be visible on her forehead. It seemed pointless to deny it.

'I'm going to betray you,' she said. What right had he to make her feel sorry for him? He was a devil. Hadn't he tempted her to do wrong all along the way? Mightn't she now be a thief and worse, if she'd listened to him? 'I'm going to betray you!' she shouted, 'and there's nothing you can do about it, is there? If you couldn't even open a door by yourself, you can't do much, can you? You needn't think I'm going to do your dirty work for you! So what *can* you do? Nothing!'

She turned and ran down the street. Deverill stood looking after her. He made no attempt to follow.

Seven o'clock on Tuesday evening. Cassie and her mother were alone in the seance room. Mr Roberts was expected in half an hour.

'Do I look all right?' asked Mrs Palmer.

'Yes. Fine,' said Cassie absently. They were ready too early, of course. Washed and brushed and sitting around with plenty of time to get nervous. 'I can smell burning,' she added.

Her mother disappeared rapidly into the kitchen, coming out a moment later, shaking her head.

'It's nothing in there. Are you sure? Can you still smell it?'

Cassie sniffed. 'I don't know. No, I don't think so.'

'Good.'

They were silent for a moment. Mrs Palmer looked once more into the mirror for reassurance. She was wearing her second-best dress. Purple. Pity she'd had to sell her gold brooch, it would've cheered it up. Funny how nervous she felt. Had she put on too much powder? She always thought a medium ought to look pale – it seemed tactless to show too much blood in the presence of spirits . . .

'Mum, I can still smell burning,' said Cassie.

They went all over the house, looking, sniffing, but could find nothing.

'*I* can't smell anything,' said Mrs Palmer. 'Perhaps there's a bonfire outdoors.'

Cassie opened the back door and looked out. There was a mist coming up, and the air smelled wet and clean. No burning.

'I must've imagined it,' she said.

'You're not nervous, are you, love?'

'A little bit.'

. . . A road stretching ahead. White mist swirling

in the headlights. Dark trees retreating rapidly on either side. The car is travelling fast . . .

'Cassie!' said her mother sharply. 'What's the matter?'

Cassie shook her head to clear it.

'I must've fallen asleep,' she said. 'I was dreaming I was in a car.'

'Poor child,' said her mother gently. 'You look tired out. Didn't you sleep last night?'

'Yes. Far as I can remember. Perhaps I'm sickening for something. How long before he comes?'

'Another twenty minutes. If he's on time.'

'I wish he'd hurry. I hate waiting. I'll be glad when it's all over.'

'Me too, love.'

. . . A road again. A side street in a town. The lights look red and blurry. The fog is thick here. Parked cars show briefly on either side and vanish. The fog ebbs and flows like a pale sea. Now the car appears to be driving into a luminous wall, now –

A dark figure! A dark figure in the headlights! Caught – no, the headlights swing wildly away. A loud crash. Metal crumpling. Twisting. Tearing. Pain, pain, pain, a smell of burning, a smell of burning . . .

Cassie screamed!

'Cassie! What is it? What's the matter?'

'We've got to stop him!' Cassie cried desperately. 'Mr Roberts, we've got to stop him! It's Deverill! I shouldn't 've taunted him. He's thought of a way, the devil! He just had to step out. We've got to stop Mr Roberts or he'll be –'

'Cassie,' said her mother helplessly. 'He'll have left long ago. He's coming from London. He's due here in ten minutes.'

'London. He'll be on the London Road,' said Cassie, running out of the door, out of the house, with her mother following. 'I've got to stop him!' she shouted over her shoulder. 'Before he turns off the main road. There might be time!'

She was running, leaving her mother far behind, hearing her mother's voice in the distance.

'Cassie! Cassie! Cassie!'

Now there was only the sound of her own breathing, and her footsteps slapping on the damp pavements. Please God, please God, please God, make me in time!

Down Chaucer Avenue, Marlowe Drive, turn right, cross into Spenser Street. Her footsteps beating a rhythm on the pavement, please God, please God, please God, make me in time!

Now the fog began to confuse her feet, seeming to lengthen and shorten the pavement at will, so that she stumbled and her rhythm was broken. A pain stabbed at her side. Her breath ached, was deafening, roared in her ears. Nearly there. Blake Road, cross into –

Oh God! It was she! Caught in the middle of the road. Caught helplessly in the headlights of a car. Like in her vision, only now on the wrong side. And as in her vision, the headlights swing wildly away.

The bulk of a car passes her so closely that she feels the displaced air like a slap, and thinks for a moment she's been hit. A loud crash, the sound of metal tearing as the car runs into a parked car and appears to be trying to climb on to its back. Its engine is still running – a smell of burning, a smell of burning.

The car is tilted at an angle. The driver's door hangs open and a figure, cradled in a safety belt, bulges towards the road. Her fingers are fumbling at the buckle before she has time to think. The smell of burning is sharp in her nose. Smoke is coming from under the bonnet, how long – how long before –

The buckle gives way and the man tumbles against her. Putting her hands under his armpits, she tries to drag him clear. He's too heavy, too heavy.

A man pushes her aside.

'Here! Let me! You take his legs. Quick! Before the tank goes up!'

She has her back to it when it explodes. The heat glows on the back of her neck, and the face of her helper turns a rosy red.

'Thank God we were in time,' he says, smiling at her.

'Is he dead?' she asks. 'Is he dead?'

Seventeen

Mr Roberts was not dead. She had known he was Mr Roberts, there was no need for the envelope to fall out of his pocket when he was being carried. No need for it to lie face upwards on the damp pavement, with her mother's writing plain in the light from the burning car. He was Mr Roberts and she had done this to him. Not Deverill. *She* had done it. *She* was the dark figure in the headlights. *She* had caused the crash. *Why?* She had only meant to warn him.

'Is he badly hurt?' she asked a woman who was bustling past carrying blankets. There were many people now, drawn out of their houses by the light of the fire.

'No, dearie, I don't think so,' said the woman kindly. 'Best not to move him too much before the ambulance comes, though. Just in case.' She peered at Cassie. 'Are you the one who saved him? Did you see what happened?'

'No,' said Cassie, backing away into the shadows. 'No, I'm not the one who saved him.'

I'm the one who nearly killed him, she thought, watching from the other side of the road. People, now outlined sharply against the flames, now blurring in smoke, were piling blankets around Mr Roberts as he lay on the pavement. Hadn't he moved? Yes, he was turning his head. Don't look this way, thought Cassie, don't look at the girl who did this to you.

Conceited idiot that she was, why had she ever gone to the cemetery? Because she wanted to show them! Mum and Tom and Mary. Show them how clever she was! Show them she could do better than her mother, she, the youngest, the seventh child! No wonder she had got Deverill. It was no more than she deserved. But poor Mr Roberts! Thank God it wasn't worse. Thank God he was still alive.

Deverill stood by her side, watching her. Flames from the burning car seemed reflected in his dark eyes.

'Why?' she asked him, miserably. 'I thought it was you, the dark figure. But it was me. Me all the time. *I* did this. I only meant to warn him. Was that wrong? What's the point of second sight if it doesn't give you a chance?'

'How can we tell what's meant to happen,' he said gently. 'Perhaps you did a good thing by stopping him. Perhaps he wasn't intended to reach the end of his journey. Perhaps that would have been the tragedy.'

'He's Mr Roberts,' she said, unable to believe he did not know. 'From the Psychic Society.'

'You were going to betray me,' he said sadly. 'Why? I was your friend.'

'But you're a devil, aren't you?'

'I don't know!' he shouted, suddenly furious. 'I don't know what I am! How should I know? Did you think I was given instructions? *You* brought me here, that's all I know. A child! Do you think I haven't wondered why? I try to serve you and you laugh at me. Offer you treasure and you refuse it. What do you want of me?'

'I want you to go away. Back where you came from.'

'No, not that,' he said, quite definitely. 'I had bad dreams. You can't ask that, child.'

'I *am* asking it.'

'And I'm refusing.'

Baffled, they both stared at the fire. The second car had caught alight now, and people were pushing another out of the way. Mr Roberts was sitting up, swathed in blankets, sipping a cup of tea, waiting for the ambulance.

'A girl ran out in front of me,' she heard his voice say. 'Right in front of me.'

A couple of men looked round, peering, as if trying to find her in the shadows. She and Deverill walked silently deeper into the fog. What was she going to do with him? He was her devil. She would have to do something. He was dangerous, she knew it now. He might not have caused this accident yet she still felt that somehow he was at the bottom of it. The sense of danger, of urgency had not ended with the accident but seemed to be growing. If only she could think clearly.

'Why is everything always so mixed up?' she asked, 'so many questions without answers, so many people believing opposite things? I thought when one died, one would know everything. But you seem as much in the dark as me.'

'The grave is a very dark sort of place,' he said, with the glint of amusement she couldn't help liking, much as she now distrusted him.

What was she going to do with him? Whom could she turn to? Whom could she ask for help, without putting them in danger?

'You called me up. This must be between us two,' he said, reading her thoughts too easily. 'You and I. Do you think you are the stronger?'

She put her hands to her head; then jumped nervously, for she seemed to hear Tom's voice ringing faintly in her ears.

'Cassie! Cassie! Cassie!'

'Can you hear anything?' she asked Deverill nervously.

'Yes. A boy's voice calling your name,' he gave her a reassuring smile. 'Not in your mind, poor child, have you been taught nothing? Two or three streets away. Coming quickly.'

'It's my brother. It's Tom.'

'Then I must go. We will meet later, in the cemetery, where we first met. It must be so. It is the time. The moon is full again behind the clouds, and the fog is clearing.'

Did he think she was a fool? Yet a voice inside her seemed to be saying, yes, yes, yes.

'When?' she asked.

'In two hours – at ten. That was the time when we met.'

Did he think she was mad enough to agree? Was he trying to hypnotise her? And was he succeeding?

'Yes,' she agreed helplessly, 'I'll come.'

Tom's shouts were louder now, and she could hear his footsteps running. Deverill stood looking at her for a moment, then the wind blew the fog over him and he was gone.

Tom came round the corner and caught her arm.

'Cassie! Thank Heavens I've found you. Mum's been frantic! What's all this about Mr Roberts? She said you'd gone to stop him on the London Road. Told you she'd come this way, Mary! Oh, damn it, now Mary's vanished. Mary!'

'Never mind Mary. Tom, you've got to help me. There's not much time. I agreed to meet him in the old cemetery at ten. It's Deverill,' she said as Tom stared at her in disgust.

'Oh, not *that* again!' he said.

'But – but – she stammered, 'didn't Mum tell you? About my second sight coming at last? About my seeing the accident before it happened?'

'Shut up, you fool,' he whispered fiercely, looking around him, 'do you want to be put away?'

'You can't think I'm mad,' she protested. 'Look –' She swung him round and pointed, 'see that red glow down there? Well, do you? I'm not just imagining it, am I? That's a car burning. Go and look if you don't believe me. And that's the ambulance,' she added, as the familiar wailing started in the distance, 'coming for Mr Roberts.'

'Cassie, what have you done?' he asked in horror.

She tried to see his face but it was dark and she could not see it clearly.

'Tom, please help me. You've always been the one to get us out of trouble. You've always thought of something. We've got to beat him or something terrible may happen. Please!'

'Pull yourself together! You're hysterical!' he said angrily. 'You need a doctor, not me! Shut up about it, will you!'

Cassie stared at his familiar, solid bulk in the misty dark.

'You're afraid,' she said slowly.

'Tom! Cassie!' It was Mary's voice coming out of the fog. Neither of them answered her.

'I just can't believe you,' he said, sounding desperate. 'I'm sorry, I just can't.'

'You can't believe me because you're frightened of spirits,' she said. 'That's why, isn't it?'

'Cassie, you're *mad*!'

'Oh, go away, Tom,' said Cassie, crying. 'Go to the McTodds!'

'Cassie!'

'*Go away!*'

'All right then. If that's what you want.'

Cassie stood, staring after him, and wiping the back of her hand across her cheeks. She could hear two pairs of footsteps, his receding and the others running towards him. Mary. Now she could hear them talking, although she could not distinguish the words. Mary would comfort her. Mary would never let her go to the cemetery alone. They could walk home together, arm in arm, back to the warm little kitchen, where Mum would be waiting, with hot soup perhaps, and baked beans on toast. She was cold and she was hungry and she was frightened. Only a lunatic would go haring off to meet a devil in a cemetery for some sort of final combat. 'Do you think you are the stronger?' he'd asked, and the answer to that was horribly easy – 'No'. She'd done her best and she'd made a mess of things, and now she was going home. She took three steps forward, and then stopped.

It was as if there was a rope attached to her back, between her shoulders, and it was being pulled the other way. A voice was in her head, telling her to go to the cemetery. Tonight, tonight, when the power was with her. Her gift was a chancy fluctuating thing, by tomorrow it might have waned. It might never come again. She had raised Deverill, and she must not leave him loose in the world.

Still she hesitated. Was it her gift speaking, her gift which her mother had always assured her was God-given. Or had Deverill really hypnotised her? Her mind seemed full of fog and she could see no way of telling. It was in the cemetery that she had raised Deverill. Perhaps only in the cemetery could the end come, his or hers. She would have to trust her gift. It was all she had, that and the seed of an idea.

'Cassie!' called Mary.

And Cassie was off into the fog, running the other way, as fast as she could. She knew Mary would never catch her. She'd outraced her many a time.

Eighteen

It was late, soon it might be too late, and still she was the wrong side of the cemetery wall. First there had been an old man looking for his lost dog. Two steps and he would stop, gazing with sad old eyes into the mist.

'Lovey! Lovey!' he called, but no-one came. Two more steps. 'Lovey! Lovey!' No answer. Sighing, he stopped and fumbled in his pocket for his pipe. With slow fingers he struck the match, and the wind blew it out. Three times the wind blew out his matches. 'Lovey! Lovey!' His voice went pleading down the street, but no dog came.

Then a pair of fat, middle-aged women panted up the hill and stopped for breath; then having found their breath, wasted it away in gossiping. This was a shame, that was a crying scandal, and *she*, whoever she was, should be ashamed of herself.

Now a pair of lovers leaned against the wall, wrapped in the mist and in each other's arms. Silent, motionless, beautiful, they might have been enchanted. Perhaps they would kiss for a hundred years while Cassie fretted in the shadows. She thought she might climb the wall unnoticed, but when she walked softly towards them, she saw the girl's eyes, wide open, were watching her over the man's shoulder. Cassie hesitated, and the girl stopped kissing to say, 'Get lost!'

'It's a free country.'

The man turned round. There was no love in his eyes.

'Go on! You 'eard 'er! Scram!'

As Cassie did not move, he raised his arm in a threatening gesture, but his girl caught hold of his wrist.

'Oh, come on, Bill. It's late, anyway,' she said, and they began to walk slowly away, hugging each other close, forgetting Cassie. She watched them out of sight. The road was empty. Quickly, by brick and ivy, she pulled herself up on to the wall.

High above in the night sky, the moon shone cold and dim. The low mist shifted over the graves like an eiderdown over restless sleepers. Only here and there was it pierced for a moment by a tall cross or the dreaming head of a stone angel; which vanished as the wind blew and the white mist rolled on. No time to lose. She had work to do. The wind plucked at her and she gave herself to it, dropping down to the hidden ground below.

Now the pale moon looked incuriously through the mist as she ran from grave to grave, calling softly, urgently, chanting the invitation to the spirits:

'Come to me! Oh, come to me! I am ready! I am waiting!'

She was calling them all. No matter that the carved names were obscured by the night: she remembered them well. Robert, the Poor Prisoner, Rosie of the two cherubs, Michael, the beloved husband, John Arthur, beloved son, even Charlotte Emma Elizabeth Webb. She was calling them to her aid against Deverill. What could she, mere flesh and blood, do against a dark spirit? She needed help, and who better to help her than the kindly respectable spirits who lay all around her? For they were not like Deverill. They were all mourned: the beloved wife, the beloved husband, the beloved son or daughter. People had cared for them when they lived, and paid to have them rest in peace when they were dead. Not like Deverill, the outcast, the unbeloved.

'Come to me, please come to me!' she called, but no-one came.

Perhaps they were resting too peacefully to hear her. Perhaps having slept for so long, they had no wish to be disturbed now. Sobbing, she hammered with her fist on a stone slab as if knocking at a door.

'Wake up! Wake up! I need you!'

The wind sighed, and the mist rose up from the graves like breath in the cold air. Crouching by the stone slab, she trembled and watched. . . . People, or spirits – a pale procession that rose from the ground and stirred, stretching, turning their heads as if half asleep, murmuring amongst each other plaintively.

'Oh!' breathed Cassie, and it was as if she had blown them away, they dissolved into the mist and were gone. Leaving only one figure, holding in its hand a lance or spear, coming slowly towards her as if wading through a white sea, and turning its head this way and that, as if looking for something. It was not Deverill. It was not tall enough and too broad. It was a knight come to her aid, a champion to save her.

'Here!' she called, and the figure started nervously, nearly dropping his spear, and stood rooted to the ground as if in terror. They stared at each other through the mist. What sort of champion was this who looked so afraid?

'Who's there?' it challenged in an uncertain voice.

'Tom!' cried Cassie, and half laughing, half crying, ran to her brother's side. 'Did you see them? Oh, did you see them?'

'See who? Can't see a bleeding thing in this damn mist! Where's his grave gone?'

'Deverill's? Why? What are you going to do? What's this?'

'A stake to drive through his heart!'

Tom, the practical one, who could not face more than one world at a time in case he fell between and was lost, who was afraid to believe in ghosts, had after all loved her enough to come with his home-made lance to save her.

'It was all I could think of,' he explained, as she

clung to him. 'Isn't that right? Isn't that what you have to do?' Proudly he showed her how he had fixed a metal point to the top of the wooden stake in case the coffin were not entirely rotted away, so that it could pierce the lid to impale –

'No!' cried Cassie. 'No, Tom!'

I am your friend, Deverill had said often. I only want to serve you . . . I had bad dreams, you can't ask that of me . . .

'What else is there to do?' Tom was whispering, looking nervously over his shoulder.

'I don't know,' she said, and shuddered. What else was there to do?

'Where's his grave?'

'This way,' she said, stumbling through the mist, feeling it cold and wet on her cheeks like tears. Would it hurt him? Would it be the end of Deverill for all eternity?

'Hurry, hurry! It's late!' said Tom. 'Let's get it over with. Where's his grave?'

As if in answer, the mist parted and there it was. Black, crooked, like the man who leaned upon it, one hand on either edge of the stone.

The children stopped and clung together in fear, and Deverill looked at them sadly with his dull black eyes.

'Are you come to destroy me, child?' he asked. 'Is that what you want?' They could not answer. He came from behind his headstone and stood before them. 'Destroy me, then!' he shouted, and tore apart his cloak and shirt so that his chest was bare. 'Strike! Kill! Destroy!'

Tom raised the stake in his hand.

'Kill! Kill! Kill!' whispered Deverill, as the boy hesitated, his face white and wet in the moonlight, the metal point of the stake quivering like a candle flame. 'Tell him, child, tell him to kill!'

'No!' Cassie flung herself at Tom so that the stake leapt out of his hand and clattered against a headstone. 'Don't you see? He wants us damned like him! Devil! Devil! Devil!' she screamed as Deverill began to laugh. Looking desperately at the graves around them, she called above his laughter, 'Come to me! Please come to me! I need you! I need your help!'

As before the mist stirred and rose up from the graves, higher and higher, forming a pale ring around Deverill. He turned this way and that, like a hunted animal, and it seemed to Cassie that the mist was taking the shape of hounds closing for a kill. Now Deverill seemed to shrink – a small dark figure, a trapped beast, a boy.

Suddenly it changed before her eyes. The night and the fog were gone. There was a village green, lit by the sun of a different century. A boy with a disfigured face and a crooked shoulder was cringing before an angry crowd. His face was wet with tears and his whole body shook with fear. The crowd was neat, clean, respectable, but their faces were as hard as stone. No pity showed in any eye, only fear and suspicion and hate. There was a sound of murmuring like the wind in the trees, that grew louder and louder until it broke into separate words.

'That's her son! Filthy little warlock! Cast him out! He'll bring us bad luck, the son of Satan! Take that, you varmint!'

A woman leaned down, picked up a stone and threw it. She missed the boy, but more stones followed, and soon the dirty, pock-marked little face was streaked with red.

'Burn him! Burn the ugly little devil!' a man shouted. 'Burn him like that damned witch, his mother!' They began closing in.

'Don't! Don't hurt him!' cried Cassie, in pity and dread. The boy, turning his head frantically, did not seem to see her. He whimpered in terror. He was completely surrounded. There was no way out.

'Here! This way!' shouted Cassie, holding out her hands to him, moving backwards to break the ring and leave him an opening through which to escape. 'Come with me! Come to me, Deverill, come!'

The wind blew, the mist rose in a white wave and washed away the figures, leaving only Deverill standing sharp and clear in the moonlight. He was again as she had first seen him, except that now his eyes were brilliant with tears and shone like the moon. He smiled at her, and lifted a hand in farewell.

'Goodbye, dear child,' he said, and was gone. There was only the moon and the wind, and the quiet graves.

Nineteen

It was the end of the haunting of Cassie Palmer. Deverill was gone. 'Gone to earth,' as Tom put it.

Cassie spent the morning in bed while the rest of her family tip-toed heavily about the house.

'Let her sleep,' she heard her mother say, and then Mary's voice, a little peevish,

'She's not an invalid, is she?'

'You don't understand. The poor kid is drained. People never realise the expense of psychic energy . . .' Their voices dwindled down the stairs.

The expense of psychic energy, thought Cassie drowsily. The cost of her gift . . . She was smiling as she drifted back to sleep and her dreams were happy, as if she thought she and Deverill had somehow got away without paying.

She came down to lunch, still in her dressing-gown, and was given the best piece of chicken, the brownest roast potato, and the top of the milk on her tinned pears. No-one complained it was unfair. She now sat, somewhat bemused, conscious of a warm glow inside her that was nothing to do with the food she had just eaten.

'I'm proud of you, Cassandra,' said her mother. 'Yes, proud of you, love.'

Cassie smiled and blushed, looked modestly down at the tablecloth. She felt like a juggler, who, having carelessly thrown too many plates in the air, finds to his astonishment that he has them safe in his hands again. Nothing was broken not even Mr Roberts' head. He was doing nicely, the hospital had assured her mother, and was fortunately to be discharged that afternoon, saving them the expense of sending flowers.

'Yes, you are a credit to your family, love,' Mrs Palmer went on, nodding her head as if in agreement with some ancestors only visible to herself. 'We are all proud of you. Aren't we?' she asked, turning to Tom and Mary.

'Yes,' they said obediently. They sounded a little as if they had been rehearsed. There seemed to be a conspiracy of admiration.

Nice as it was, she couldn't help wishing the brave young clairvoyant, whose deeds her mother was now describing, bore a little more resemblance to the Cassie Palmer she knew herself to be.

'Oh Mum,' she thought, hanging her head, 'I'll never be able to tell you. It wasn't like that at all. I thought mostly only of myself. I wasn't concerned with helping a poor, lost spirit, but just with getting rid of him. I couldn't help liking him, but I thought he was a devil.'

'. . . A spirit that a grown medium might've shrunk from,' her mother was saying. 'For let's face it, Cassie, he was no oil-painting, was he?' . . .

Poor creature. Could she have helped him better if she'd been older? She remembered how he'd said, 'You called me up, you, a child! Do you think I haven't wondered why?'

Yet I did help him in the end, she thought with pleasure. Me, Cassie Palmer, thirteen years old. In spite of my faults and all the mistakes I made. Perhaps it had needed a child . . . She had seen him fixed, like a butterfly on a pin, to an old terror; caught for the rest of his life and the next two hundred years. Then she had stumbled along, and somehow, together, they had found a way out.

She was glad. She supposed, with training, she could learn to help other spirits. But she would much, *much* rather be a doctor and help people when they were still alive.

She wondered if she had any choice. What sort of doctor would a clairvoyant make? Bandaging fingers three days before they bled, or treating last year's germs when the patient was already recovered. Had she any right to turn her back, refusing help she was better qualified to give? Perhaps there *was* a price ticket on her gift. Perhaps she was going to have to pay with her whole future.

Her mother was standing now, holding the tea pot in her two hands, almost as if she was about to present it to Cassie as a prize. She said,

'You need never be ashamed of the way you used

your gift. You used it well. You used it bravely. Helping that poor, unhappy creature was a fine achievement! Something that for the rest of your life you can look back on with pride and pleasure.'

'Mum, you sound as if you were going to give me a clock and pension me off,' said Cassie.

To her surprise, her mother blushed. She fidgeted. She put the tea pot down and clasped her hands together, almost as if she was praying for something. Possibly inspiration.

'Cassie, Oh, dear! My poor love, I don't know how to tell you. We – we have a saying in the family: early come, early go. Try not to be disappointed. Your gift, it came too sudden and too strong. It does sometimes at adolescence, and when it does, it burns itself out. I may be wrong – no! No, I mustn't deceive you. I'm not much of a medium nowadays but when I get a certain feeling here,' she thumped herself gently on the stomach, 'I'm never wrong. Never! I'm afraid it's gone, love. Try not to mind. Remember it ended well. Burns bright, takes flight, as we say. And it's something to have burned brightly, if only for a little while.'

'Poor Cassie,' said Tom, before she could speak. 'So young and already a has-been.'

'You shut up!' shouted Mrs Palmer, turning on him furiously.

'Mum, I don't want to be a medium! I never did! Not really!' said Cassie, laughing. 'I want to be a doctor.'

'Why the devil couldn't you have said so before,'

said Mrs Palmer, exasperated. 'I've been awake half the bleeding night trying to think how to break it to you. A doctor! My word! A doctor! Well, why not? I suppose anything is possible now.' She sounded dazed.

'I'd have to get grants and holiday jobs.'

'Don't you worry about that side of it. You just work hard and pass your exams.'

'But how will you manage?'

'Without your help, d'you mean, love?' asked her mother, laughing. 'Bless you, ducks, I'll be all right. We'll find somewhere to live, and then you watch! Madame Palmer will be back in business again as large as life. We'll manage. Nobody's ever got me down for long.'

'Poor old Mum,' Mary said later, as she and Cassie were going to bed. 'She put a good face on it, didn't she? All these years looking forward to your precious gift, and when it comes, you waste it all on some dusty old spirit in the cemetery. She can't even send him a bill. And we could do with the money.' She looked rather pointedly at her sister.

'I know what you're thinking about,' said Cassie.

'Do you?'

'Deverill's treasure.'

'Right first time. Well?'

'That sweet shop will have gone by now.'

'No it hasn't. I rang up the Estate Agent and asked.'

'There'll be nothing there.'

'Probably not. But we can look, can't we?'

'I'm not breaking in.'

'Who said anything about breaking in?' said Mary, sounding shocked. 'You leave it to me.'

'You'll have to pay for that lino,' said the old lady. Her name was Pettifeather, and her pug's name was Otto. Otto was trying to help them, scrabbling with his paws, snuffling enthusiastically and getting in their way.

'All right,' Cassie agreed rashly.

'But only the top layer,' added Mary. For beneath the brown lino in the attic, there was green lino.

'Hidden treasure, that's a good one!' said the old lady. She began wheezing with laughter, sounding so like her dog that at first Cassie thought it was an echo. She didn't mind being found a joke. At least the old lady had let them in and agreed to their searching. That was thanks to Mary. Mary had a way with old ladies. She liked them and they nearly always like her.

Beneath the green lino, a faded rose-patterned lino –

'Remember, the treasure's mine,' said the old lady, wiping her eyes with her handkerchief. 'My house, my treasure!'

Cassie stopped working immediately.

'Half yours, half ours!' she said indignantly. 'We agreed. We shook hands on it.'

'That was before I knew where it was,' said the old lady slyly. 'Haven't got anything in writing, have you?'

'We trust your honour,' said Mary. 'A nice old lady like you.'

'If you find anything,' said Mrs Pettifeather, beginning to shake and wheeze again, 'you can have it all, my dears.'

'Half yours, half ours,' said Cassie firmly. Beneath the rose-patterned lino, there was newspaper. Old, yellowed, crumbling beneath her fingers.

'Here! Don't tear it! Give it to me,' said the old lady. She took the pages gently in her aged, shaking hands and began to read. The girls went back to their work. A loose floor board but where? Lord, they were filthy! Their hands were already black. Carefully Cassie poked and prised with her knife.

'You can't take the whole floor up,' said the old lady. 'Careful, my girl! You're splintering the wood. I can't afford –'

'This one's loose!' Cassie was trembling with excitement, and the pug, catching it from her, jumped round them, yapping.

'Otto! Sit, good boy, sit!'

There's nothing here but dust, Cassie told herself, preparing herself for disappointment. She noticed that Mary's eyes were full of tears, as if she too was preparing for the worst. Slowly she prised the board up. Darkness, dust, nothing, nothing but a box, a blackened box covered with rotten sacking and dirt. There was silence in the attic except for the sound of breathing. Two girls and an old lady and a pug looked at the box and then looked at each other.

'Open it,' whispered Mrs Pettifeather. 'Open it.'

'I can't!' stammered Cassie. 'I can't! It's stuck.'

But the lid flew open and clattered to the floor. The covering cloth ripped easily under her fingers, and there it was! Gold coins mostly, a little silver, a small pearl brooch . . . Deverill's treasure.

Now the attic was filled with noise as the old lady and the two girls started capering about with glee, clapping their hands, and kissing each other and laughing, while the little dog ran round in circles making the most noise of all.

In the old cemetery, the headstones lean sleepily, the grass grows long and wears feathery plumes nodding in the sun, and there are only wild flowers: dandelion, and ragged robin and the white trumpets of convolvulus. Except in front of one grave, where someone has planted forget-me-not. This headstone is black with age, speckled and pocked with grey, with one corner angling up sharply like a crooked shoulder. It says simply: Deverill. 1720–1762. And underneath, carved unevenly but with love, the letters:

R.I.P.

Also by Vivien Alcock

THE STONEWALKERS

'*Poppy, dear girl, she told herself, shutting her eyes tight and beginning to tremble, you may be the biggest liar out of hell, but you're not so far round the bend that you can't see both ways.*'

Poppy isn't mad – the statue Belladonna really has come to life with the lightning flash. But Poppy Brown *is* a liar – so who will believe such things could happen – and worse, that the statue is a vengeful, furious creature, not the smiling friend Poppy once thought her?

A brilliant and chilling story.

THE TRIAL OF ANNA COTMAN

Thin, sallow and nosy, Lindy Miller is the most unpopular girl in the school. They only let her join the Society of Masks because she was Jeremy Miller's kid sister. When a new girl arrives, the quiet, smiling Anna Cotman, Lindy persuades her to join the Society too. Originally set up to combat bullying, the Society of Masks has become a sinister power group run by bullies. When the gentle Anna challenges their rules, the leaders decide to make an example of her and the terrifying countdown to the day of her trial begins.

Vivien Alcock captures the chilling mood of evil let loose in a school when childish rituals run out of control.

Also by Vivien Alcock

GHOSTLY COMPANIONS

It was the last straw. Furiously, he reached out and snatched off her mask.

'Oh God!' he screamed.

But what was it that he saw?

A collection of ten ghost stories written with Vivien Alcock's superb skill in blending the natural and the supernatural. A figure-head that is more than it seems, a patchwork made like none other, a mirror image that never leaves you alone, a garden that no child should enter at night, a masquerade that gives you the chance to be someone else . . . The settings vary from the familiar local Common to the exotic atmosphere of Venice while the moods vary from the funny to the frightening. A feast to satisfy all tastes by a master storyteller.

THE SYLVIA GAME

Emily's relationship with her father, an unsuccessful artist, is tinged with mistrust since the bailiffs visited the family home. When he takes her on holiday to Devon and goes out on 'business' for a day, Emily therefore decides to follow him.

Losing the trail at the entrance to an old stately house, Emily comes into contact with Oliver – and discovers a connection between herself, her father and the mysterious Sylvia Game . . .

A Selected List of Fiction from Mammoth

While every effort is made to keep prices low, it is sometimes necessary to increase prices at short notice. Mandarin Paperbacks reserves the right to show new retail prices on covers which may differ from those previously advertised in the text or elsewhere.

The prices shown below were correct at the time of going to press.

☐	7497 0978 2	**Trial of Anna Cotman**	Vivien Alcock	£2.99
☐	7497 2388 2	**Whispers in the Graveyard**	Theresa Breslin	£3.50
☐	7497 1794 7	**Born of the Sun**	Gillian Cross	£3.50
☐	7497 1066 7	**The Animals of Farthing Wood**	Colin Dann	£3.99
☐	7497 2384 X	**Granny was a Buffer Girl**	Berlie Doherty	£3.50
☐	7497 0184 6	**The Summer House Loon**	Anne Fine	£2.99
☐	7497 1558 8	**The Apprentices**	Leon Garfield	£3.50
☐	7497 1784 X	**Listen to the Dark**	Maeve Henry	£2.99
☐	7497 0136 6	**I Am David**	Anne Holm	£3.99
☐	7497 2387 4	**The Phantom Piper**	Garry Kilworth	£3.99
☐	7497 1664 9	**Hiding Out**	Elizabeth Laird	£3.50
☐	7497 0791 7	**The Ghost of Thomas Kempe**	Penelope Lively	£3.50
☐	7497 1754 8	**The War of Jenkins' Ear**	Michael Morpurgo	£3.50
☐	7497 0831 X	**The Snow Spider**	Jenny Nimmo	£3.50
☐	7497 1772 6	**The Panic Wall**	Alick Rowe	£3.50
☐	7497 0656 2	**Journey of 1000 Miles**	Ian Strachan	£2.99
☐	7497 0796 8	**Kingdom by the Sea**	Robert Westall	£3.99

All these books are available at your bookshop or newsagent, or can be ordered direct from the address below. Just tick the titles you want and fill in the form below.

Cash Sales Department, PO Box 5, Rushden, Northants NN10 6YX.
Fax: 01933 414047 : Phone: 01933 414000.

Please send cheque, payable to 'Reed Book Services Ltd.', or postal order for purchase price quoted and allow the following for postage and packing:

£1.00 for the first book, 50p for the second; **FREE POSTAGE AND PACKING FOR THREE BOOKS OR MORE PER ORDER.**

NAME (Block letters) ....

ADDRESS ....

....

☐ I enclose my remittance for ....

☐ I wish to pay by Access/Visa Card Number ☐☐☐☐☐☐☐☐☐☐☐☐☐☐

Expiry Date ☐☐☐☐

Signature ....

Please quote our reference: MAND